READER BONUS!

Dear Reader,

As a thank you for your support, Action Takers Publishing would like to offer you a special reader bonus: a free download of our course, "How to Write, Publish, Market & Monetize Your Book the Fast, Fun & Easy Way." This comprehensive course is designed to provide you with the tools and knowledge you need to bring your book to life and turn it into a successful venture.

The course typically **retails for $499**, but as a valued reader, you can access it for free. To claim your free download, simply follow this link ActionTakersPublishing.com/workshops - use the discount code "coursefree" to get a 100% discount and start writing your book today.

If we are still giving away this course by the time you're reading this book, head straight over to your computer and start the course now. It's absolutely free.

READER BONUS!

ActionTakersPublishing.com/workshops
discount code "coursefree"

Stories of Perseverance

NEVER GIVE UP

Email: lynda@actiontakerspublishing.com

Website: www.actiontakerspublishing.com

ISBN # (paperback) 978-1-956665-40-6

ISBN # (Kindle) 978-1-956665-41-3

Published by Action Takers Publishing™

Dedications

This chapter is dedicated to anyone who is learning their triggers and dealing with abuse of any form. You are braver than you believe, stronger than you seem, smarter than you think, and loved more than you know.

~Adra Shamika Nicole Glenn

I would like to thank my husband for supporting my biggest dreams, even when he couldn't see them.

My daughters for sacrificing time with me so that I could pave the path and create the best future for them, and all generations that follow.

My sister for following me on all of my adventures; from multiple cross-country road trips, to creating a business and helping me raise my daughters. Her love and support haven't waivered and I'm lucky to have a sister who I can also call my best friend.

My dearest lifelong friend, Pamela, who has been by my side through thick and thin; births of children, heartbreaks, losses of loved ones, and every day in between. My words can't describe my gratitude for our soul connection.

~ Cindy Taylor

I dedicate this chapter to my Mum Valerie. Mum had many health challenges during her lifetime, many strokes, the last one was too severe. Mum taught us to never give up, stay strong, give it our best and keep smiling.

~Jacalyn Price

I dedicate this chapter to the University Women's Caucus. As a result of the fellowship of women, I learned the value of saying no. I also dedicate it to my husband, Andre, who has supported me and stood by me through many challenging times.

~Kimberly Adams Tufts

To my mother, Alberta Banks, who has always believed that I can do anything. I feel her love and concern for me even when I am nowhere near.

~Kimberly Robinson

To my loving family, Dave, Paige and Brendan.

~Kinga Hipp

To all educators and teachers who are seeking to find the 'right' environment to provide the 'right' guidance for their students. You all deserve the very best.

To all our Learning Success Coaches who have taken the leap to be 'an agent of change.'

To all my 1600+ students who were my guides and inspiration and who helped me to get to where I am today.

To my son, Jay, who always tagged along with me during all my struggles and was always there to pick me up when I needed it.

And to all my mentors, including my husband and business partner Rod Bellamy, the first person to notice that what I was doing was beyond tutoring and that I was serving from an empty cup.

~Kohila Sivas

I dedicate this chapter to my beautiful, wonderful, loving family. They are the reason I do all that I do.

~Latara Dragoo

To all those who helped me thus far to reach this beautiful place on my life journey, I thank you.

~Laurie Bodisch

In memory of my mother, Susan. In honor of my sons, Kaden and Owen. You are my reason for never giving up.

~Melissa Kimmerling

I dedicate this chapter to my amazing boys, Soheil and Raiden, who keep me grounded and always striving to be a better mom. May you continue to grow and flourish as you were meant to, soaring with the eagles. I love you, my babies.

~Najia Said

I dedicate this chapter to my mom, Florence (Ossie) Larkin. She is one of the most selfless women I have ever met and she would move mountains for her children and grandchildren. She gave me my creativity and taught me how to be a mom and teacher.

~Sally Green

This chapter is for my darling daughter who inspires me every moment.

~Sally Ross

This chapter is dedicated to my husband, Stuart. Without your support, I couldn't have made it through this difficult journey.

This chapter is also dedicated to all Breast Cancer Warriors - no matter where in their journey they are. May this chapter inspire everyone.

~Susan Beam

I'm grateful to the Lord for opening doors I thought were closed to me... for granting miracles affirming my path. I'm also thankful for the amazing women He brought into my life... women who chose to walk with me on this journey. They always encourage and support me, with many having truly become the sisters I never had.

~Susannah Dawn

Dedicated in loving memory of my son, Sean. I will carry on his legacy by helping others. Sean unexpectedly passed from this life, March 15, 2023. Sean loved to dance and sing and was involved in the Special Olympics in basketball skills and ramp bowling. Sean knew everybody and will be remembered for being a friend to the world.

~Teresa Dawn Johnson

I dedicate this book to my amazing girls, Avery Jewel and Sophia Madison, who inspire me to be the best mom I can be every day because you deserve nothing but the very best. I adore everything about the two of you and love you with all my heart and soul!

I also dedicate this book to my dad, Ronnie Roper. I am me because there was you. Thank you for being exactly the Dad I needed so I can be the mom I am. I stand on your shoulders and will always look up to you for wisdom.

~Tiffiny Roper

To my precious daughter, Joanna, who has taught me the true meaning of unconditional love. Your determination, resilience, and kind heart never cease to amaze me. This chapter is dedicated to you - may it inspire you to embrace the possibilities life offers.

~Virpi Tervonen

Foreword

Throughout my career as an athlete, I have come to understand that the journey to achieving greatness is not an easy one. It requires a lot of dedication, hard work, and most importantly, perseverance. Perseverance is the quality that distinguishes successful people from those who give up when the going gets tough.

As I reflect on my own experiences, I can't help but think about the countless obstacles and challenges I had to overcome to become a four-time Olympian in the Luge. There were times when I felt like giving up, times when I doubted myself, and times when I wondered if all the effort was worth it. However, what kept me going was my unwavering commitment to my dreams and my belief that anything is possible if I never give up.

That's why I'm honored to introduce you to *Never Give Up: Stories of Perseverance*. This book is a compilation of inspiring stories about individuals who refused to let setbacks and obstacles stop them from achieving their dreams. Each story is a testament to the power of perseverance and the human spirit.

The stories in this book come from a diverse range of individuals, from entrepreneurs to ordinary people who have faced extraordinary circumstances. Yet, despite their different backgrounds and experiences, they all share a common trait - the unwavering determination to never give up. Their stories are a testament to the fact that no matter how tough the circumstances may be, anything is possible if we are willing to put in the hard work and never give up.

As you read these stories, you will be inspired by the resilience of the human spirit. You will be reminded that it's not just about what happens to us, but how we respond to it. Each story in this book is a reminder that we all have the strength and the courage to overcome any obstacle that stands in our way.

For me, this book is not just a collection of stories but a source of inspiration. It reminds me of the importance of never giving up on my dreams, even when the odds seem stacked against me. It reminds me that success is not just about talent or skill, but about the will to keep going when things get tough.

I am confident that this book will inspire you, too. Whether you're an athlete, an entrepreneur, or just someone who is trying to achieve your dreams, these stories will show you that anything is possible if you are willing to persevere.

I want to take a moment to commend the authors for putting together such a wonderful collection of stories. They have captured the essence of perseverance and have presented it in a way that is both inspiring and insightful.

Lastly, I want to encourage you to read this book with an open heart and an open mind. Let these stories inspire you to never give up on your dreams, and let them remind you that anything is possible if you are willing to persevere.

Thank you for choosing to read *Never Give Up: Stories of Perseverance*. I hope it inspires you as much as it has inspired me.

Ruben Gonzalez
4X Olympian, Author, Speaker
TheLugeMan.com

Table of Contents

See the opportunity, then seize the opportunity.
~Lynda Sunshine West

A Winning Note From Lynda Sunshine West and Sally Green

Welcome to "Never Give Up: Stories of Perseverance." Within these chapters, you'll embark on a journey through the extraordinary lives of 23 individuals who have chosen to defy the odds, overcome obstacles, and embrace the power of unwavering determination. These stories stand as a testament to the human spirit's ability to triumph in the face of adversity.

From the realm of entrepreneurship to the world of creative arts, each author's narrative is a vivid reflection of the transformative journey they've undertaken. As you delve into these tales of resilience, you'll discover that setbacks are not barriers but opportunities for growth. The path to success, often marked by twists and turns, is an intricate tapestry woven with the threads of perseverance.

Compiled by Action Takers Publishing, this anthology is a celebration of the strength that resides within us all. The contributing authors share their own journeys of facing fears, transforming challenges into stepping stones on their path to empowerment. Their experiences remind us that no dream is too ambitious and no obstacle insurmountable.

"Never Give Up: Stories of Perseverance" is an invitation to embrace the indomitable spirit that propels us forward even when faced with the most daunting of challenges. Whether you're an entrepreneur navigating the complexities of business, an artist seeking to channel adversity into inspiration, or an individual on the quest for resilience in everyday life, these stories will kindle the flames of determination within you.

As you embark on this literary journey, remember that giving up is not an option. Instead, let these stories inspire you to persevere, to push past your limits, and to uncover the remarkable strength that resides within. Let's embark on this odyssey together, exploring the boundless potential of the human spirit as we navigate the landscapes of perseverance and triumph.

Lynda Sunshine West and Sally Green

CHAPTER 1

From People-Pleaser to Empowerment Advocate

Lynda Sunshine West

In the ever-evolving mysteries of my entrepreneurial journey, I've discovered that challenges are not setbacks; they're the catalysts for growth. My name is Lynda Sunshine West, and I stand as the Founder & CEO of Action Takers Publishing. Embark with me on a deeper exploration of my eight-year odyssey within the realm of bestseller book publishing – a journey that's been marked by transformation, resilience, and a relentless pursuit of empowerment.

Eight years ago, when I embarked on this adventure, I had a cloudy vision. I thought I knew what I wanted and what I was going to do, but I was wrong. One of the greatest lessons I've learned along the way is that no matter how clear I am today, I may meet an incredible person who teaches me something new, which gives me new clarity. The quest for clarity never ends.

My journey started with quitting my 49th job working in the corporate world for 36 years. I worked my way up the proverbial corporate ladder and landed job #49 working for a

Judge in the Ninth Circuit Court of Appeals. I had worked my ass off to get there. I was a legal secretary for 20 of those 36 years and worked at seven different law firms (climbing the ladder to new heights along the way).

I was so excited when I got that job working for the judge. "I made it." I was on top of the world. Until I wasn't.

You see, just like the previous 48 jobs, I was looking outward for what was inside of me, but I didn't believe in myself enough to see it. I was seeking outward approval.

I quit every single one of those jobs.

I

am

a

quitter

At least that's what I believed about myself for decades.

At the age of 51, I hired a life coach who took me down a different path, a path of self-discovery. I had a LOT to learn about myself. I was instilled with the beliefs that, "I am stupid. I am ignorant. People are only nice to me because they feel sorry for me. I am worthless. I have no value." The list goes on. Unfortunately, you probably get what I'm saying.

So many of us believe that we aren't worthy. Why is this? I have my own opinion that I'm going to share with you.

We are all born into an environment filled with beliefs. Mom, dad, grandma, grandpa, brother, sister, friends, babysitter, teacher, you name it, we are indoctrinated with other people's beliefs the moment we are born.

Then this happens.

We either believe them or not.

We either adopt their beliefs to be our own or not.

For some of us, the negative beliefs are false and they are used as fuel to create success. We choose not to believe what they said. It doesn't become our truth.

For others, the negative beliefs become our truth and we live our lives as who "they" said we are. We have a hard time not believing what they say about us. It IS our truth.

Why are some people wired to shake off the negativity and say, basically, "Screw you. You can believe that about me all you want, but I'm not going to be that person. I choose to be different than what you say about me." While others absorb it and live their lives with that truth, "Okay. If you say that's who I am, that's who I will be. You're right."

I was the latter. I believed all of the negative words that were said about me. And I lived it as if it were true. I can't even begin to imagine what my life might be like if I hadn't believed all of the negative things that were said about me.

The roots of my life trace back to a pivotal moment from my childhood. At the tender age of five, I embarked on an impromptu week-long journey, venturing away from home. Yeah, I ran away at five years old. This escapade, though seemingly trivial, sowed the seeds for a lifelong belief. I believed for decades that they didn't come to get me because they didn't love me and didn't want me around. I ended up coming home with my tail between my legs, became riddled with fear, and turned into an amazing people-pleaser. That early encounter with fear became a cornerstone for my evolution, propelling me from a timid people-pleaser to an audacious advocate for empowerment.

My personal journey to conquering fears didn't truly begin until I turned 51. I embarked on an extraordinary mission: to confront one fear each day for an entire year, aka The Year of Fears. This transformative odyssey reshaped my identity. It metamorphosed me from someone plagued by self-doubt to a fearless warrior who approached challenges with unwavering courage. The confidence and strength that stemmed from this year-long feat of daily bravery became a cornerstone of my entrepreneurial identity.

As an entrepreneur, my path extended beyond business strategies; it delved into the realm of storytelling and transformation. My passion for both learning and teaching culminated in the creation of a proprietary system that streamlined the often daunting process of book publishing. I wasn't merely a CEO overseeing operations; I was a guide, walking authors through a journey that was efficient, enjoyable, and empowering. It was about more than publishing a book; it was about orchestrating a transformative experience through the written word.

My journey, however, wasn't limited to business and work; it encompassed my personal passions. It was at the age of 47 that I decided to embrace music, particularly the bass guitar. This musical venture, fueled by an unquenchable passion, culminated in creating a rock band called Useless Rhetoric with my husband. It was a living testament to the philosophy that age was not a barrier to pursuing new avenues of growth. This musical voyage paralleled my entrepreneurial journey; both required a willingness to step beyond my proverbial comfort zone and embrace uncharted territories.

The culmination of my journey found expression in my book, *"Do It BECAUSE You're Scared."* This literary creation wasn't just a collection of words; it was a roadmap to transformation. The 7 Simple Steps outlined in the book encapsulate the very principles that empowered me to conquer my own fears. It isn't a theoretical manual; it is a testament to the power of facing fears head-on and emerging stronger on the other side.

Beyond the pages of the book, though, my journey was fueled by a larger purpose: the goal of empowering 5 million women and men to share their stories with the world to make a greater impact on the planet. That's how Action Takers Publishing was born, out of my love to empower others to share their stories. It's in our stories that we have our greatest power. Our stories transform lives. Our stories give hope where there once was none. Action Takers Publishing isn't just a platform for publishing; it is a conduit for change. Each book we publish becomes a vessel of transformation, contributing to the collective journey of empowerment.

Collaboration forms the very heart of my approach. My background as an Executive Film Producer and Red Carpet Interviewer expanded my horizons, allowing me to connect with a diverse range of individuals who share my zest for life. This extended reach facilitates connections that extend beyond the realm of publishing, forging bonds with like-minded souls on a journey of growth and self-discovery.

My journey isn't defined solely by successes; it's also marked by the challenges I have navigated along the way. The path I tread hasn't been a linear one; quite the contrary. It's a mosaic of moments – moments of fear, moments of triumph, moments of transformation. Action Takers Publishing isn't just a business venture; it's a testament to my unwavering commitment to fostering empowerment and change.

As the sun dips below the Californian horizon, painting the sky in hues of gold and indigo, I find myself immersed in reflection. The fears I confronted, the barriers I shattered, and the community I nurtured were all integral chapters of a story that is still unfolding. Action Takers Publishing isn't just a company; it is a legacy, a testament to my steadfast dedication to empowerment and transformation.

My chapter in this book stands as a tribute to an entrepreneur who dared to dream, dared to face fears, and dared to build a community rooted in collaboration. It's a reminder that within each of us resides the power to surmount challenges, embrace change, and script our own narratives of triumph. As the journey continues, each page turns, revealing a story characterized by resilience, growth, and an unwavering pursuit of empowerment.

Lynda Sunshine West

Lynda Sunshine West ran away at 5 years old and was gone an entire week, came home riddled with fears and, in turn, became a people-pleaser. At age 51, she decided to break through one fear every day for a year and, in doing so, she gained an exorbitant amount of confidence to share her story. Her mission is to empower 5 million women and men to write their stories to make a greater impact on the planet. Lynda Sunshine is the Founder and CEO of Action Takers Publishing, a Speaker, 28 Times #1 International Bestselling Author, Contributing Writer at Entrepreneur Magazine and Brainz Magazine, Executive Film Producer, Red Carpet Interviewer, and Summit Host.

Lynda Sunshine believes in cooperation and collaboration and loves connecting with like-minded people.

Connect with Lynda Sunshine at www.ActionTakersPublishing.com.

CHAPTER 2

Hi Mom

Sally Green

During the weekend before Thanksgiving of 2019, my brother called me with heartbreaking news: "Mom has Alzheimer's." Despite my belief that I was emotionally prepared to hear those words, the reality struck me harder than anticipated. Witnessing her memory loss, the confusion, and the increasing difficulty in everyday tasks - they all pointed to something being wrong. My brothers and I encouraged her to seek medical advice, but nothing could prepare me for the definitive diagnosis. The weight of those words hit me like a tidal wave, leaving me stunned and struggling to comprehend the enormity of it all.

It was a devastating blow that shattered my world. My mother was my best friend. As days turned into years, I watched her gradual decline and the agonizing descent into the merciless clutches of this unforgiving disease. I felt helpless as I watched Alzheimer's mercilessly strip away her memories, her independence and, ultimately, her recognition of her family members. This is my story dealing with the effects of Alzheimer's - a story woven in love, loss of memory, and the indomitable bond shared between a mother and her daughter.

While my mother found happiness in her own world (shaped by the grasp of Alzheimer's), the rest of us, especially my father, struggled. She was and still is my best friend, my biggest cheerleader, and one of the most selfless women I have ever known. I witnessed my mother's personality slowly diminish. Her once vibrant mind became clouded, and even the simplest tasks - like balancing the checkbook and cooking - became obstacles. As bill payments became a challenge, I assumed the responsibility of managing my parents' finances.

In the early stages of her diagnosis, my mother's personality remained largely intact. We would talk daily on the phone, reminiscing about cherished memories, sharing laughter, and enjoying each other's company. But as the disease tightened its grip, her spirit began to fade, replaced by confusion and disorientation.

In the years that followed, her conversations grew fragmented, accompanied by the onset of hallucinations and escalating paranoia. My morning telephone calls became a delicate dance, attempting to reassure her that the weatherman on the television wasn't sitting in her kitchen. Until one day, when the telephone calls stopped altogether. During all this, there are still these tiny moments when she shows her true self, even if just for a moment.

Alzheimer's demanded sacrifices—my mother's ability to care for herself, her independence, and the future she and my dad envisioned together are gone. It is a relentless thief, robbing her of the simplest joys: our morning coffee chats on the telephone, making her favorite recipe, planning birthday parties for the grandkids. With each passing day, I witnessed a part of her slipping away, like pages torn from a cherished book.

One of the cruelest aspects of Alzheimer's is witnessing the person you love no longer recognizing you and your family. Each time my mother doesn't remember a family member, it shatters my heart a little more. It is a bitter pill to swallow, but I cling tightly to the precious memories of family gatherings, the stories we shared, and the immense love my mom had for all of us. Even if she doesn't remember, I still do.

Even though my mom is still alive, she doesn't understand when I talk to her. Since her diagnosis, I have made huge changes in my life. I became a multiple-times bestselling author, was offered (and accepted) a job as Vice President of a publishing company, created and taught online courses, have been invited to speak at online events, and so much more! It's been such an incredible journey, but here's the thing... it's bittersweet because I haven't been able to share any of it with my mom. So, I thought I'd use my chapter in this book as an opportunity to share the morning chats I would have had with my mom, had she not become ill.

==

March 2020

Hi Mom,

Today was a really bad day and I'm in a bad place. When I looked in the mirror, I saw what a mess I was!! With all this covid talk, one of my customers called and canceled us and money is already tight. Then, I stepped on the scale. I know I shouldn't have done that, but it made me realize I need to lose 80 pounds. What am I going to do?

I went for a walk in the cemetery with Billy and Amanda. We only walked for 30 minutes, and I was totally out of breath. When I came home, I threw away all the junk food. I'm going to start eating healthier. I was wondering, do you have any good low-calorie recipes? Also, I hate listening to all the negative news on television, so I'm turning it off and taking some online marketing classes. I'm going to start investing in me!

July 2020

Hi Mom,

I have already lost 40 pounds. Last night, I was up late and stumbled upon a Facebook live session with Forbes Riley. She offered everyone listening to the opportunity to contribute a chapter in her upcoming book *"1 Habit for Entrepreneurial Success."* I became Facebook friends with her after purchasing her Spin Gym product on QVC a couple of years ago. To my surprise, she accepted my friend request! Out of all my Facebook friends, she is undoubtedly the most famous. I woke up early this morning and wrote my chapter. I'm going to join the book. I have always wanted to be a writer.

October 2020

Hi Mom,

Guess what, that book I wrote a chapter for became a #1 International Bestseller on Amazon! The other authors and the publisher are telling me that I can now introduce myself as a bestselling author! I am so excited. Anyway, they are going to interview me on Zoom and ask me about the book. It will be my first time ever being interviewed. I'm going to put on makeup and curl my hair. There are some other famous people in this book, too. It's exciting. I have met some of them in the Zoom meetings. I really don't think I belong in this book, but I want to be friends with all these people. They are all so nice. I'm going to go through the book this weekend and send them all friend requests and see what happens.

January 2021

Hi Mom,

I had so much fun in that first book that I am going to do it again. This book is called, *"1 Habit to Thrive in a Post-Covid World."* I have connected with so many amazing people in both books. One of the authors invited me to attend her weekly online networking meetings. I've been attending every Saturday. Her name is Lynda Sunshine. You would really like her. So many of the people I've met are life coaches. I have no idea what a life coach is or what they do, but I'm going to hire Lynda Sunshine to help me create a coaching program. Wish me luck.

March 2021

Hey Mom!

I'm working with Lynda Sunshine on my coaching program. I'm calling it, The Self-Care Rockstar. It's all about helping women take better care of themselves, just like I did. This week she approached me about writing chapters in two of the books she's putting together. It sounded fun, so I said "yes!"

Oh, and get this! I applied to speak at an online summit, and can you believe it? They accepted me as one of the speakers! I have no clue what I'm going to talk about. Honestly, I don't even think I'm any good at this. But hey, I have a meeting with Lynda Sunshine coming up, and she's going to guide me through it all.

April 2021

Hey Mom,

I'm going to start an online show on YouTube where I interview people in the self-care arena. I'm calling it The Self-Care Rockstar Show. I have never interviewed anyone before. I created a post in Forbes Riley's group asking for people to interview and three people reached out to me. What do I do now?? I was going to delete the post because I'm afraid. What if nobody watches, what if I look stupid? I spoke with Lynda Sunshine and the women inside our mastermind. They all encouraged me to not give up. So, I'm going to do it.

September 2021

Hey Mom!

Guess what? I am on a roll with this writing stuff. In less than a year, I've contributed chapters in four different collaboration books, and get this - they all became #1 International Bestsellers! It's been such an exciting journey.

You know Lynda Sunshine? Well, we have become really good friends. One day I noticed that she seemed really stressed and I offered to help her. I have been helping her with her website, graphics, and marketing for the two books she just launched. Then yesterday, she called and asked me if I wanted to partner with her and expand her book publishing business. Can you believe it? Of course I said "yes!" We changed the name to Action Takers Publishing! I'm going to be a book publisher! How cool is that?

Oh, and I'm not going to host the Self-Care Rockstar show anymore. I have learned so much in the past 5 months interviewing people. In addition, it was a lot of work putting it all together and I had no idea how to monetize it. I want to devote all my free time to the publishing business.

February 2022

Hi Mom,

Lynda Sunshine and I published our very first book together! The book is called *"Wellness for Winners"* and it went above and beyond my expectations and even became a bestseller on Amazon. Working with all the authors was so much fun - I loved hearing their inspiring stories and creating this book has been extremely rewarding. I contributed my own chapter and wrote about my self-care journey.

I can't even begin to describe how happy this work makes me. Right now, it's just a part-time gig, but Lynda Sunshine and I have big dreams of turning this into our full-time careers.

I absolutely love the publishing business and I can't wait to see what exciting things the future has in store. We're all about making a positive impact in the world and we're super pumped about the journey ahead.

November 2022

Hi Mom,

Guess what? I'm headed to Las Vegas! I'm beyond excited because I'll finally have the chance to meet Lynda Sunshine in person. We are hosting a writing workshop while there. We will be staying at an Airbnb. As you know, it's been over 26 years since I last flew on a plane, and this will be my first time ever flying alone. I'm embracing all these new experiences, which are both exciting and a little bit scary!

I've been doing lots of live interviews with authors lately. And let me tell you, when I first started, I was bad at it. I had no clue what questions to ask and would stammer all the time. There were even a couple of times when my brain just froze, and I would, umm, or stop right in the middle of a sentence. But you know what? I didn't give up, practice makes perfect, right? I'm not going to give up and I am going to keep learning all I can. Lynda Sunshine is a great teacher.

March 2023

Hi Mom,

I'm really pumped because I'm heading out to San Diego for this awesome event called Secret Knock with Lynda Sunshine. You won't believe it - she is going to be one of the speakers! This is a tremendous opportunity for us to establish and promote our publishing business, making it more recognized and reaching a bigger audience. I can't wait to hear the speakers and connect with the other people in attendance. Super excited about it all!

July 2023

Hi Mom,

Want to know something cool? Lynda Sunshine and I launched four books in June! That makes a total of nine this year. I'm now an 11-time #1 bestselling author.

We have been working hard. A few times a week, Lynda Sunshine and I hop on Zoom meetings and work on the business. We call them work parties. Sometimes I will look at the clock and realize it's 2 am and we have been talking and planning for hours. It's been a lot of work, wow, we've made so much progress and I'm learning a ton. I hope you're proud of me!

==

While writing this chapter, I was surprised at the surge of emotions that surfaced. Typically, I'm not emotional or one to shed tears. However, during the writing process of this chapter, I cried.

To those who have loved ones battling dementia and Alzheimer's, please know that I see you, I feel you, and I hear you. I know how tough it is. When faced with a family member's cognitive decline, it's easy to focus on the losses: memories fading, abilities diminishing, and witnessing the person you once knew slipping away. However, I want to encourage you to maintain a "Never Give Up" attitude and tap into an unwavering spirit of resilience that allows you to find strength in small victories. It's about finding joy in the present and cultivating gratitude for what you still have.

But it's not just about caregiving; it's also about taking care of yourself. You can't pour from an empty cup, so it's important to seek support from others, whether it's family, friends, or a support group. Asking for help is not a sign of weakness; it's a necessary step to ensure your well-being and the well-being of your loved one. I am lucky to have friends and a big family to talk to and draw strength from; many people are not that lucky.

Alzheimer's may steal memories and abilities, but it cannot diminish the love and connection shared between family members. Celebrating moments of clarity, sharing a laugh, or cherishing a tender gesture become precious treasures through the storm. My "never give up" attitude helps me to find joy and gratitude in these fleeting moments and encourages me to focus on what remains rather than what is lost. My mom may not remember, but I still do.

And remember, you're not alone on this journey. There are others who understand what you're going through. Together we can support each other and make a difference. By sharing our experiences, raising awareness, and supporting research, we can work towards a future where Alzheimer's has less of an impact and, hopefully, a cure.

So, if you're feeling overwhelmed or on the verge of giving up, hold on to that "never give up" attitude. It's a powerful force that can help you weather the storm and find the strength you didn't know you had. You've got this. Let's face Alzheimer's head-on.

The Storm

By Sally Green

The storm you face is fierce, but storms -- they never last.
You are an overcomer, have faith that this will pass.

The pain and fear is real, you're a fighter, you are strong.
Be still and gather courage, say a prayer and move along.

This isn't WHO YOU ARE, but a journey you must take.
The road ahead looks rocky, you're tired and you ache.

But others have survived this, be determined you will, too.
Take a helping hand when offered, let others
help you through.

You're beautiful and tough, take my hand let's run this race.
God's plan for you, it far exceeds - the circumstance you face.

Sally Green

Sally Green is the Vice President of Author Development at Action Takers Publishing. She works with writers to help them develop their stories and become bestselling authors. She is a Christian educator and bible study leader. In her spare time, she enjoys painting and teaching acrylic paint classes to local senior centers, Women's groups, and Children's summer camps.

At the age of 58, Sally realized that she was really good at taking care of everyone else, but really bad at taking care of herself. So, she embarked on a journey of self-care that began with investing in herself and contributing to a multi-author book. Sally is an inspirational speaker, a multiple-times International Bestselling Author, and has written three bible studies. She is in the process of writing her own book.

Connect with Sally at www.ActionTakersPublishing.com.

CHAPTER 3

Getting to Know Your Triggers

Adra Glenn

Knowing my triggers was something I had to learn when growing up, and now also. I really didn't know anything about trigger points, boundaries, or what abuse really was. It took me having anxiety attacks, dealing with depression, dealing with abuse of all forms, getting a good therapist, setting boundaries, and never giving up to really see what my triggers were. When I was younger, I grew up seeing my mother and other family members being abused. At the time, I didn't realize this wasn't okay. We were told to go into our rooms or go outside while things like that were going on. We couldn't talk outside the house about what went on in the house. Welcome to my life. I hope my story helps you if you are having issues with setting boundaries or going through some form of abuse.

I was born in 1977 to a woman that was very strong-minded, got things done, and didn't allow any disrespect. As a child, I watched my mom have gatherings with family and friends. They would be having good conversations, laughing, and dancing. It would just be all smiles on everyone's faces. She had male friends, and most were nice.

This one man I remember very clearly was not so nice. I remember him putting his hands on my mother quite often, and it got to the point that we had to leave home in the middle of the night often. We would go down to my granny's house, which was like two miles away. Sometimes we would get in; sometimes we wouldn't. The nights that we couldn't get in, we had to walk back home, hoping Mr. Man was asleep and didn't have the door locked or blocked. I remember my mother telling me to be very quiet when getting back home. Those nights, she would sleep in my room with me; we called it having a sleepover. So, as you see, I saw domestic violence at an early age and really didn't know what it was.

At the age of five, my mother and I walked over to my grandmother's house to visit with other family members. I believe my grandmother was at church. Remember I told you my mother didn't allow any disrespect? Because of this, my mother and my grandmother's neighbors didn't get along. I remember this so clearly. My mother was combing my hair on the porch, and this lady just kept picking on my mother, so eventually, they got into an altercation, and my mother was stabbed, which led to her passing away from internal bleeding. I remember going to the funeral, and when my dad and I went up to the casket, I got to give my mother one last kiss and couldn't understand why she was so cold. Then, things just didn't make sense.

This is where things got crazy and weird, but I was shown love from family, friends, neighbors, and church members. I moved in with my grandparents and went with my father and my other granny on weekends and summer breaks. At this point in my life, I could have given up on everything, or they could have given up on me. Losing my mother was so confusing to me; I didn't understand it. I was lost at times and still am to this day.

I felt like I was a burden on my granny. Her kids were all of age, almost grown, and here I came, making her start all over with a five-year-old child. My father had other kids, but I was the only one by my mother. The first time I saw my father cry was after the passing of my mother. I think he was in love with my mother. I listened to the stories my family would tell me about them. The only thing I could do was hold him and tell him we would be okay. At the age of five, what did I know about everything being okay? I'm guessing that's what you are asking. Well, I just knew we would. I had a village and didn't realize it till I was in my late twenties. My and my father's bond got to be stronger, and I'm so thankful for everyone that helped raise me, especially my granny. She was so strong. At this point in her life, she had buried three out of six of her own kids.

Life was back to normal for me. I was going to school, playing at the community center, going to church, modeling, doing pageants, you name it. My granny had me in a lot of different activities that kept me busy and active. I also believe this kept me from thinking about the tragic loss I had just gone through. I remember I would get in trouble if the house wasn't clean on Fridays when my granny got off work. When I got home from school, she didn't care what was on my schedule. That house had better be clean when she hit that door at 4:30 p.m. If not, my butt was in the house for the night.

Let's fast forward to the age of fourteen when I met this gentleman. Yes, he was older than me, like seven years older. What was I thinking? I guess that is what you are asking. Well, I didn't know his real age at first. Then, when I realized his age, I was in love with him. Now I call it young, dumb, and full of cum. Back then, I thought I was in love. Baby, whoever thought it was wrong, I thought they were just jealous and didn't want to see me happy. Baby, you couldn't tell me anything when it came to this man—he was my god. He was one of the D Boys in the neighborhood that had a fancy car, jewelry, cell phones, clothes, and shoes—if you know, you know. I was wearing name-brand items that I didn't even know about. I also didn't know what came along with all the glam.

The abuse!

We started talking, and one thing led to another, and we ended up in a full relationship. I ended up getting pregnant and having my first child when I was fifteen while I was still going to school. Back then, the high school I was in actually had daycare, so it made it much easier for me to be able to stay in school.

The abuse got worse. It got to the point that I wasn't able to be in certain people's presence, and I couldn't be in the same class, ride the same bus, or eat lunch with people that he thought liked me or I liked. Or if he heard anything, I would get physically abused. After he beat my ass, he would have sex with me and take me shopping, then send me home. This happened several times.

I recall one time when we were going to a drugstore. We were sitting in the car, and I was looking at something out the window when all of a sudden, my head hit the window and my jaw got knocked out of place. I don't remember doing anything for him to hit me. In all reality, do we ever do anything for someone to hit us? Most of the time, it's them dealing with inter issues.

The car next to us had someone sitting inside, and when I looked up, they were asking if I was okay and had a shocked look on their faces. I could only hold my face and cry and ask why. I believe people knew what was going on but feared him. I believe the neighbors could hear him beating me and me just screaming for help. I don't know where his mom was when this was going on, but she was never there when he did this. This happened several times on several occasions.

I ended up getting pregnant with my second child by him about a year and a half later. So, when my second child was born, things got harder. I could no longer take the boys to the school daycare. I had to figure out how to get a babysitter for one and then leave one at the school. I had no help from the dad; he had nothing to do with me or the kids at this point. He was still more concerned about me being in someone else's presence at the school. When it came to taking care of my kids, he didn't; he wouldn't come to anything concerning my kids—birthdays, holidays, nothing.

When you take all the domestic, verbal, mental, and emotional abuse, and the neglect of his kids, it was a lot to deal with. It's all abuse in some form. So, when he found his next girlfriend (victim), I was out of the way and was caring for two kids alone and learning how to get things done and figured out. This is another reason I could have given up, but I had to keep going and fighting. I had my two sons to live for. This is when I tell you that my grannies, father, family, and friends stepped up even more. Without them, I don't know if we could have made it. So, at this point, I had two kids, stayed in the projects, was in school, on public assistance, and lived with my grandmother. Trying to find a job was not an option with two kids.

I started talking to another man I went to school with. He stepped up and took care of my kids as if they were his own. His family was great and loved me and my kids. But I found myself back in a relationship where I was getting cheated on and lied to—he had other kids on me. This is a form of abuse whether we realize it or not. In this relationship, things had gotten really toxic.

So, when I turned eighteen, the kids and I moved out from my granny's. I thought it was going to be better and this man would stop cheating. Well, that was wishful thinking because he didn't! By me moving away, I got away from one abuser to deal with another one and different types of abuse.

When you are in an abusive relationship—whether it's mental, physical, emotional, or verbal—abuse is abuse!

I found myself in a revolving door trying to find childcare and living in the projects and on public assistance. I was dealing with depression and anxiety. Not knowing I had been dealing with it or what it really was, and not knowing my triggers, I started self-medicating by drinking and smoking herbs—if you know, you know.

Dealing with depression and anxiety, at times, I felt like this was helping, till I had a bad anxiety attack. My attacks were more like me having Tourette's symptoms. That's when my family told me I hadn't had one that bad since my mother passed.

I ended up in a relationship with someone and found myself living in Memphis, Tennessee, with my kids. Yes, I moved three hours away! Left furniture and all. The kids and I were gone, and I didn't tell anyone. My family was looking for us, and when they finally found us, I was wanted by the police in Nashville for questioning. That's another story for another book. So back to Nashville. I got on the Greyhound bus with my kids during a very scary time for me. Here goes this revolving door I told you about—a single mother of two kids on public assistance at this time applying to get back in public housing. That's one thing I can say—I wasn't scared to take risks.

I ended up meeting my third child's father and marrying him. Yes, your girl got married in her living room at nine months pregnant, working at McDonald's, and on public assistance. When I said this relationship/marriage was no different, it wasn't. Coming into the relationship, we had issues. This man was lying, cheating, and had women calling and coming by my house, flattening tires, busting windows out of my cars, pouring sugar in my gas tank, putting batteries in my gas tank—you name it, it was done. And this man had multiple kids on me.

Talking about abuse, it was like I couldn't catch a break. At this point, I thought I was a magnet or had a sign on my forehead stating that abuse was welcome here. My depression and anxiety got worse, and let's add trust issues in there. He ended up going to jail, so there I went again with single motherhood, with three kids now.

I enrolled in school to be a CNA. This was a thirteen-week program. This was where I started to find my passion. I love taking care of elderly people and listening to their stories. Still to this day, I'm a CNA and business owner of a home care agency licensed by the state of Tennessee.

At this point in my life, I started dating women. Yes, women. Dating women was different. It involved more emotions and feelings than dating men. Women like to talk and show their emotions and affection more than men. Now, did I think this was going to be different in a good way? Yes. Was it different? No! It doesn't matter what gender you are dating when you are dealing with any type of abuse. It's *not* okay! Abuse is abuse! It is okay not to be okay!

My official diagnosis was anxiety and depression, and I was given prescriptions for antidepressants and sent on my way. Throughout the years, I have been on and off my medications. There were times when things got too much for me to handle. I wouldn't know what to do but shut down, get in my bed, and just lie there in the dark for days at a time. That's because I didn't know my boundaries or recognize my triggers.

Oh, but now—baby, I can recognize my triggers and know my boundaries. I started seeing a therapist who showed me ways to set up boundaries and notice my triggers. Sometimes I must have a "come back to Jesus talk" with myself because I let other people's problems bother me. That's when "Don't worry 'bout it, sweetheart" comes in. I think I can fix or help everyone.

By me knowing what my triggers are, I remove myself from a lot of situations now. Some people may think it's me being mean or antisocial, but at this point in my life, I don't care what people think or say. I must do what's best for me. I only get one shot at this thing called life. So far, it has been a great life. I have been through so much and learned so much, and I didn't give up. I'm glad I didn't because I wouldn't be here today to tell my stories.

It's okay to remove yourself.

It's okay to go see a therapist.

It's okay to set boundaries.

It's okay to live your life like you want.

It's okay not to be okay.

Adra Glenn

Adra is a mother of three children, Glam-ma of one, and owner and founder of Caring with Love Home Healthcare, ASG Tax Service, and ASG Dispatching LLC.

Adra spends most of her time caring for others. She cares for special needs clients in her home, while still making sure her family and friends are spending time and making wonderful memories together. Adra loves to help, mentor, and lead people in the right direction with starting their own businesses. Adra's passion is caring for and looking out for others.

She also thinks she can fix everything, and her favorite words are "Don't worry 'bout it, sweetheart." Adra is also someone you can call to always be that listening ear and tell you the route you should or shouldn't take in your situation or refer you in the right direction. Adra is a big believer in mental health and getting counseling. Yes, counseling, or talking to a therapist, however you want to look at it. Adra will ask you in a heartbeat, "Have you thought about going to see a therapist?"

African American people think you are crazy for going or even asking about a therapist. Well, baby, Adra is a true believer that this truly helps. Adra's life, thoughts, energy, prayers, and peace are everything to her.

Connect with Adra at https://www.adra-glenn.com

CHAPTER 4

Everything Old is New Again

Caryn Isaacs

There is a saying in healthcare, to get ahead, you must quit and change jobs. I did that a lot at the beginning of my career. Now, I can say that I appreciate the opportunities I was given to learn new things and to understand who I am as a person. After working my way up from dental assistant to the front desk, to supervisor at a health insurance company, the person who was above me suggested I become a consultant. He knew that it was just a matter of time before I took his job.

I was lucky that I had a built-in pool of contacts to draw from. I knew a lot of young doctors who wanted to start their own businesses. I knew where the target population was of patients who wanted health care covered by their insurance. I had people coming to me asking for help. At the time, we all paid the doctor for each service, and you were reimbursed by your insurer. I was lucky to be at the right place, at the right time. The laws allowing advertising for professionals had just gone into effect, so there wasn't much competition.

There was no internet back in the 1970s, so I went to the Business Library and looked up organizations. I created a flyer saying that I was available to speak about patients' needs and contacted all the doctor organizations, local and national. One of the first groups to reply was the Public Health Association. They suggested that my topic fit into their work on Health Reform. I became known as an expert on health reform issues and using health insurance to build a physician practice. At that time, there was a section in the New York Times under business opportunities called physician practices. Most of the ads were for buying and selling a business, so my ad stood out for those looking to start or expand a business. I also had this special niche, where I had the contacts (or knew how to make them) to zero in on specific populations. Instead of general advertising, I offered my clients relationship marketing. I developed a questionnaire to determine the perfect patient for each doctor, the one who accepted their treatment plan, paid the fee (by using their insurance), and referred others to the practice. I asked the doctors about their personal style and their comfort level while learning new things. My services included everything from site and equipment selection to hiring and training staff, to business systems, to branding and relationship building with unions and companies.

I've had mentors who encouraged me and functioned as role models throughout my career. In those days, there weren't many women business owners, so it was hard to find someone who had the level of success to be willing to share their knowledge. I was extremely fortunate to meet Martha Stevens, a consultant who had built a physician sales business. She introduced me to the few others in the field, most like her were the wives of doctors. I was the new kid, but I was also different in that I wasn't married to the doctor, and I was part of taking healthcare in a direction that they didn't all agree with, accepting insurance and advertising. Martha generously spent hundreds of hours with me talking about pricing my services, looking the part, and balancing my private life.

One of my clients was Dental World, the home of one-day dentistry. They had an in-house laboratory, a movie theater, and babysitting. The office was in Roosevelt Field Mall, one of the largest in the area. The owners were two young guys with brains and good looks, so it was easy to sell their services. They didn't have a lot of start-up capital left for marketing, so they asked me to work on commission. I had never done that before, but it seemed like a good opportunity, and they offered me 5%. Well, 5% of nothing is nothing so I was taking a big chance, but I had done some insurance claims consulting for them before, so I trusted them and believed in the concept. The arrangement also allowed me to continue to have my own business separate from them. Before long, I was known as Miss Dental World. Representing a big company opened many new doors. We had lots of free publicity in magazines and on television. One of the most exciting things to happen was the company went public and I got to learn how that worked. On top of that, they started a franchise, and I sold one to a client who went on to play a big part in my life, more on that later.

All good things come to an end. Many offers come to businesses when they are on the way up, not all should be accepted. One day, a businessman gave the owners a ride on his plane. This led to an offer to purchase a controlling interest in the company. They were over the moon, but unfortunately, they didn't have the proper advisors to evaluate the offer and do their due diligence. Before any money changed hands, Mr. Businessman installed his girlfriend in my seat and directed me to give her all my contacts, train her and split my commissions. I would also have to report to another layer of management, who didn't like my speaking style. Well, I didn't have to be asked twice. I negotiated a buyout of my contract which did not include giving up any of my trade secrets. Within the next few months, the company went bankrupt. It turned out that

Mr. Businessman was a fraud and walked off with the working capital.

Here's where my business made a big turn. I still had all the contacts with the groups, but no product. I had spent so much time with Dental World that I had all my eggs in one basket. I went to the groups and explained that the client who had been paying to fund the programs was out of business. What to do? It was suggested that they would still collaborate with me if I found another sponsor. So, here's where the franchisee comes back into the picture. He was a dentist, but his wife was just graduating from school as a Radiologist. Even though the franchise sponsor went bankrupt, it didn't affect the ownership of the franchise, so my reputation was still good. In fact, the doctor wanted to retain my consulting services for his wife. After doing my homework, I suggested that they open a chain of radiology centers. No one was thinking of doctors as big business in those days, the early 80s. The centers they opened became a most successful business and a model for hospitals to outsource to ambulatory centers.

Over the next two decades, I built my business around improving access to healthcare by forging relationships with hospitals, large physician groups, and business organizations. I was exposed to all the new technology in medicine including MRIs and a machine that could send heart monitoring over the phone lines. I also spent a lot of my personal time learning about how health care is funded, how to price services, and giving courses to physicians about improving their bottom line by taking advantage of changes to the health system.

As the century changed, technology was giving insurers more information about what they were paying for health services. I participated in the discussions by joining committees, serving on boards, and participating in health reform activities. In the early 80s, the Postal Unions, who at that time, were the largest insurers in the country, struck a deal to offer their members the same coverage given to all Federal Employees. And in 1989, the employees of NYNEX, the telephone company on the east coast, went on strike over the demands, by the employer, that the workers' pay into their health plan. No one had heard of managed care beyond one Health Maintenance Organization where people, mostly government employees, went to a clinic for their care. Other than that, most people still paid for their care on their own and received reimbursement. The Union won the strike and NYNEX was forced to continue paying for the Welfare Fund. The unions realized that this would just be the start of givebacks demanded by employers. Spearheaded by the Physicians for a National Health Plan and other national organizations, such as the Universal Healthcare Action Network and local groups like Ralph Nader's New Yorkers for Accessible Health Care, discussions about the crisis facing people without health insurance gained a wide audience. Culminating in the Clinton Health Plan proposal, I participated in many planning groups especially those interested in a Single Payer model. I even worked with a group of my clients to start a physician-owned HMO.

Then in 2001, the World Trade Center was blown up. I had recently moved into a condominium in downtown Brooklyn, as I was setting up an ambulatory surgery center at #2 WTC for a client. My office was at 67 Wall St., just down the block. I watched the planes fly into the buildings, but we all thought it was just a fire. Once we realized that besides the buildings being gone, there wouldn't be any customers allowed in the area for an exceptionally long time, I lost that contract. We couldn't even open our windows in Brooklyn with all the smoke, and the streets leading into the city from Brooklyn were all blocked off. My mother passed away in May 2001, and I inherited her apartment in Florida. So, I moved there, and now in my 50's, I decided to investigate my own healthcare and what options there were for older adults. I continued to service my clients in New York, by phone and with the occasional plane trip. I took training as a volunteer for Medicare and offered a class to the residents of the community in Florida, bringing in speakers and helping people to understand their health coverage. People started asking me if I could help them to find a doctor, give them a ride to the doctor and help them in other ways.

One of my first paying clients was the former Mayor of North Miami. He was the person responsible for writing the condominium laws in Florida. He had suffered a stroke and received physical therapy. He looked the same as he always had, however, they thought he had lost his hearing. His trophy wife left him and his children from his first marriage didn't want anything to do with him. He asked if I could help with a new machine, he had invested in so that he could read the newspaper. I found out that he hadn't in fact lost his hearing. He was suffering from Aphasia, the same condition that Bruce Willis now has. He could only absorb three words at a time, then the words would disappear. I produced a system for him to give a speech at senior centers where we would practice the answers to some typical questions, and I would cue him as to which answer he should use. Another of my clients was the woman who had started the dietician programs in the New York City Schools. I helped her work with an attorney to fund a charity, since she had no family.

In 2004, I returned to New York. The publisher of a local newspaper told me about a membership organization made up of companies that served the senior population. I joined the Senior Umbrella Network and quickly joined the Board as Secretary of Brooklyn and Treasurer of Nassau County. I had been using the title of Patient Advocate since the inception of my business. Now, I tried to explain what a Patient Advocate does. I would tell attorneys, fiduciaries, and other service providers, for senior citizens, that when they had run out of options, then they could refer the client to me. I explained that the difference between a patient advocate and a care manager is that the care manager gets the patient to comply with what the doctor or family says, whereas the advocate listens to what the patient wants and tries to figure out a safe way for that to be accomplished.

With improved technology, insurance companies are now able to compare doctors' fees and evaluate their utilization. I tried to get the doctors to voluntarily install electronic health records, but they didn't want to spend the money. A group of Advocates even offered to review the provider contracts for an annual assessment of $75, but the doctors refused. When the insurers began to enforce the contracts, the doctors cried that it wasn't fair. I realized that patients would be caught in the middle and in 2008, I gave up collaborating with doctors entirely. Over the next few years, people started saying that they were patient advocates too, even though they weren't working in the same capacity that I was, supporting only the patient's wishes.

In the same way that I always believed in participating in the industry, not just in thinking of my own company, I joined several professional organizations for Patient Advocates. I became a mentor to others wanting to get into a private professional advocacy business. And in 2018, helped to develop a Board Certification exam for Patient Advocates. I received my Board Certification as one of the first to be allowed to use the letters BCPA after my name.

Around that same time, as a member of the SUN Queens Board, the Chair announced that she was retiring and no one from the Board was willing to step into her shoes. It required a lot of time for a volunteer position. I also knew that people who held the chair position had little ability to promote their own businesses. It was left to me and another person on the Board to let people know that the organization would have to cease operations. I was so upset; I owed a lot to this organization that had helped so many of us. I was talking to one of the members and she said that she was learning a technique called Havening and would I be willing to function as one of her test cases using the issue, of having to come to grips with the end of SUN-Q. The Havening session lasted a few hours, after which I felt much better, more secure in my decision, and less guilty about letting the organization go. Then, out of the blue, I was discussing the Havening session with an Attorney I was meeting for networking, and he said that HE would be willing to take it over. Just like that, I agreed to be his co-chair for a year. We rebuilt the organization by increasing the Board to include people who took on a lot of responsibility, so that the chair didn't have to do all the work. Then came the Pandemic! Many suggested that the organization close until the pandemic passed. But I heard about ZOOM and wondered if we couldn't meet online. Every meeting for the next two years was a huge success. People said they enjoyed the ability to talk to the entire group better than just those whom they met in person at a typical card exchange. This year, I moved on to the position of Chair Emeritus and we continue to hold meetings as a hybrid of online and in-person.

As one door closes, another door opens. I was asked to join the Board of a well-respected community organization. PULSE Center for Patient Safety, Education, and Advocacy has many programs for patients and their support persons. Once a month, I moderate one of the programs. We want you to know that if you are dealing with a health problem, you are not alone.

I always like to use whatever tools are available to assist me in my work. In one of the networking groups, I met a coach who really thought outside the box. His approach allowed me to think about what I wanted in my life, not just in my business. Another coach exclaimed when I told her who my perfect client is, "You work with ICONs." In thinking it over, I realized that I am an ICON, an Aging Icon. And my clients are ICONs.

My current clients include a 97-year-old lady who, after a career as a psychologist and probation officer, began to write plays. Her work was well-received off-Broadway and later at her assisted living facility. During the pandemic, she wrote three new plays and was despondent that all her works would be lost after she was gone. I found a theater graduate to put all her works into a website and we published the new plays as books available on Amazon. Other clients are people who have exciting, productive, interesting lives, but need some assistance due to problems related to aging or health issues. They don't need the typical home health services or to be forced into early retirement. Together, we find creative solutions.

Time flies when you're having fun. I have enjoyed my long career and can't imagine ever wanting to stop helping people and fighting for health care to be better, more cost-effective, and more accessible for all. I find ways for Aging Icons to continue their life's mission because when they say that nothing else can be done, that just means that they don't know what to do.

Caryn Isaacs

Caryn Isaacs works with a limited number of interesting, exciting, older adults who just happen to have some limitations due to aging or a health issue. She has over 40 years of experience and knowledge of everything healthcare, legal and financially related to older adults. She specializes in out of the box solutions beyond the usual services for senior living. Caryn is known for her storytelling and interactive programs that empower people to identify and overcome obstacles to reach their goals.

Connect with Caryn at
https://gethealthhelp.com.

CHAPTER 5

My Journey Back Home

Cindy M. Taylor

Chapter One: The Place That I Call Home

grew up in a small town in Wisconsin. I was born and raised on a dairy farm. I learned so many valuable lessons that no textbook could ever teach, for that I am so grateful. I was different from the others though. Being one of very few farm kids in the school immediately set my siblings and I apart from the 'cool' crowd. Luckily, I had a way of acting like a chameleon so that I could hide anywhere I went. I wasn't like the other kids who got excited about a party on a Friday night. I would have rather been home with my parents, but I remember forcing myself out of the house so many times just so that I wouldn't be the only one staying in on a weekend. I pretended to be someone I was not and after so many years, I realized, even as a young child, I was moving through the motions.

I was quiet and shy. I didn't have a voice and didn't express anything I felt. I simply wanted to be non-confrontational and keep the peace in all situations. I thought that if I agreed with everyone else, I would somehow be accepted and liked more.

I didn't realize that pushing down my voice would lead to a future without choice and without power to create my own life. It would eventually lead to a life controlled by everyone and everything else around me. The me I was born to be, was buried beneath conformity. It seemed easy as a child, but as I grew up, I realized it would take serious work to break free from this life that is in front of me.

Chapter Two: Whisked Away

I had the same friend from Kindergarten through Middle School, but then, as we grew up and personalities changed, we drifted apart.

I dated mostly older boys until my senior year in High School.

I remember it vividly. It was in Mrs. Green's Communication class, 5th period, when I struck up a conversation that would eventually lead to an 11-year relationship. I met the most charismatic boy that day that I ever laid eyes on. Something happened in that moment that would alter the direction of my future forever; one would say it was a defining moment in my life.

I wasn't sure how this quiet farm girl caught the attention of the star football player, but all I knew was I felt like the luckiest girl in the world. Except for the fact that I was tormented in the hallways by the popular girls and heard snickering for the rest of the year. I realized they were just jealous. I took the high road because I knew that he had chosen me. I only had to survive six months of the school year before graduation, so I did my best to ignore the mean girls.

None of that mattered though, because something inside of me told me I was right where I belonged, and I felt loved like I never had before. I knew we were meant for each other. We were married just a year later. To a young 19-year-old, I felt like I was living a fantasy life that only happened in the movies.

I packed up my entire life into a U-Haul truck and said good-bye to the only life I ever knew. Tears rolled down my face as we left that August day. I waved to my family and best friend in the rearview mirror and I, somehow, knew that pulling out of the driveway symbolized the ending of my childhood.

While I felt immense emotion for everything that I left behind, I was so excited for the new journey I was about to embark upon. This small-town country girl was heading for the city; we were off to San Diego, where he would serve his Marine Corp term for eight years. We enjoyed scenic travels through the countryside and had many laughs and adventures over the course of a few days.

After 2000 miles, we arrived at our final destination and our new life together. We moved into our little apartment close to Marine Corp Camp Pendleton base. Everything was perfectly decorated with our new furniture and accessories that we just received for our wedding. We were just a few steps from the swimming pool and palm trees surrounded our view from each direction. It seemed like I was a child playing house.

I went from being a teenager who couldn't drive on the highways in Wisconsin to having to navigate my way through eight lanes of traffic on one of the busiest freeways in the country. I had no choice but to figure it out. There was not a learning manual that would ever prepare one for this real-life stuff that I just jumped into. There were so many times I wanted my mom, and many instances I wanted to give up, but I knew that I couldn't. It was like I had something to prove to the rest of the world. I wanted to show that we could survive on our own and defy all the odds that stacked against us. Along came twists and turns that would soon be a foreshadow of what was to come.

When I arrived in San Diego, as luck would have it, I landed the perfect job that would soon turn into my new-found career path. I became a professional Leasing Consultant in a 5-Star resort-style apartment community. It was a fancy job where I could dress up in high heels and company-paid tailored suits. I felt like a queen.

I rose through the ranks, climbed the corporate ladder and had what I thought was the best job in the world. My office overlooked the Pacific Ocean, where I had a view of swimming pools, palm trees and the most beautiful, manicured gardens.

My family from Wisconsin visited frequently, so most months I felt like a tour guide exploring the city. From breweries to zoos, to California Adventures, I felt as if I was living my best life.

Chapter Three: Changing Plans

Just as I thought I was at the pinnacle of my career, my husband decided it was time to end his military career. This hit me out of nowhere, but I didn't have any input because he had already submitted his military discharge paperwork, and everything was already in motion. I did what I needed to do to plan our final cross-country journey back to Wisconsin.

The military packed up our condo and my husband left a month before me to begin his new career at the Police Academy. I was left behind to tie up all of the loose ends. I said my farewells to my friends who had become family through the years and my sister flew in a few weeks later to drive back with me. While my sister was there, we toured all of our favorite places and took pictures of all of the places we visited throughout the years so that I would remember some of the best days of my life. As we strolled down memory lane, it became clear that it was the ending of a very life-changing chapter. I came to California as a quiet, shy girl without a voice and would leave a confident businesswoman.

After making the journey cross-country with my sister and two cats, my husband and I settled, ironically, right back to my same childhood home. I was returning to everything I once knew nearly a decade later - my hometown, my family, my friends; back to the place I once called home.

Chapter Four: The Day Everything Changed

That was until everything I knew changed forever. Four simple words took me to my knees and I would never be the same again. "I want a divorce" are the words he uttered just a few short months after we returned.

Just as I had accepted my new life back home, everything as I knew it abruptly ended. I couldn't believe the words I was hearing. I felt like I was in a bad dream. Many thoughts crossed my mind. "Why did you wait until now to tell me? I could have stayed in San Diego where I was happy, successful and established." "Was there someone else?" "Is this just PTSD from the war?" My mind went crazy. It was as if I was paralyzed and frozen in time.

I needed to know. I wanted answers. How did this happen? How could it be happening to *me*? I wanted the truth. I had intuitions in the past of another woman; a woman whom I had suspicions about our entire marriage, but he assured me that he loved me, that he chose *me*. He would say, "You're just insecure, you have to let it go." He made me believe I was going crazy. Each time my gut sensed infidelity, I pushed it down so far, as if it didn't exist, because I could not face it. Not in my marriage, I thought.

Now I was forced to confront my biggest nightmare. My voice quivered, "Are you in love with her?" Again and again, "Are you in love with her?" He didn't answer. He remained silent. "If he wasn't, why wouldn't he just say no," I thought? Then it came: "YES". That was it. That was the last word I would ever hear him say. Three letters, one word and my world shattered into a million different pieces. It was as if someone socked me so hard in the stomach that I couldn't breathe. I sobbed uncontrollably as if my life just ended. I wanted to go to sleep and pretend none of this happened.

It was nearly midnight when he walked out the door with nothing but a backpack on and took off on his motorcycle. The taillights pulling out of the driveway symbolized the end. I wanted to run after him, chase him down as if I could catch him, then maybe I could make him change his mind.

No emotion, no explanation, no remorse. 11 years and this is how it ends. I was in utter disbelief.

I felt so alone. I couldn't tell anyone, no one would believe me. To those looking in, it appeared as if we had the perfect marriage. The perfect life. It turns out that was all just a facade.

How could I have been so blind? I felt so embarrassed. He was living a double life right in front of me and I didn't know it. How could I be so naïve? I blamed myself. I made excuses for him, like maybe it's because we got married too young and he didn't have time to sow his seeds. Maybe I wasn't good enough, pretty enough, smart enough. After all, how does a farm girl get the football star? I should have known better. The popular girls were right. Somehow it was easier to blame myself than blame him.

I didn't sleep that night and many to come. My eyes were so sore from crying that I had to put ice bags on them before going to work the next day. It took every ounce of energy to get out of bed. It was difficult putting one foot in front of another. I felt as if I was in a car wreck and my body survived, but my soul suffered a total loss. It was as if I was walking around in a body aimlessly, in a world I didn't know.

Every day seemed to get harder as I learned more and more about his lies. It turns out it was even worse than I could have imagined.

Chapter Five - Learning to Let Go

The year following that hot July evening was the worst of my life, but amidst all of the fog in my mind, I knew one thing: I would not let him win. I remember thinking to myself: Cindy, your self-wallowing is over. You now have two choices – 1. Allow this to have control over your entire life or 2. Choose to pick yourself up, rise and move on. I would not allow this to define my life.

It was a long road, but I chose the latter. I had to; I knew that if I didn't heal myself, then he would win. If I didn't forgive him, then I would be the one stuck in the past. 18 months later, I called him up and said, "I forgive you." I knew he couldn't understand it, but I knew this is what I needed to do to free myself.

I decided to be grateful for our journey together regardless of how it ended. I chose gratitude for the friendships I had met along the way. I thanked him for being in my life, for all the good times we had shared and the memories we made over the years.

I chose to see this chapter as the one that helped me instead of crippled me. I decided to see this story as the first one that cracked my soul; the one that allowed light in so that I could live a better life one day. I thanked him again and I hung up the phone.

While I knew moving to forgiveness would help me heal, I still had a lot of grief to process. As the days went on, I felt so lost, I felt so empty. I wasn't prepared to do this alone. I felt as if I was nothing without him. It was like he was my safety net, moving from my childhood straight into our lives together. I so easily molded to the life that we built together, I never for a moment created anything for myself. I simply went through the motions in life day after day. It was like I was a 29-year-old learning to walk again, learning to live again. How could I have given away my control, my entire life? How would I ever begin to build again? I was left alone to create a life out of the rubble of my past and, on most days, I wanted to give up.

It seemed so much easier to let go and be a puppet on a string controlled by people and events in life. I'd never had to think before, I just did. I rolled with the flow, and I followed the crowd. I went where he went, did what he said and somehow lost my entire identity along the way.

I remember hearing my maiden name for the first time again in nearly a decade and it took me back as if I didn't recognize who she was.

Chapter Six: Re-Discovering Me

This awakening forced me to discover myself. It made me peel back layers that I never knew existed. I immersed myself in self-help books and I read for hours and days straight. In some weird way, it gave me hope that this ugly, dark period of my life would pass quickly, and everything would be okay again.

I wanted to give up so many times. On the dark nights that I felt so alone, during the lonely moments when memories crept in. But something inside of me knew that there were brighter days ahead. As I held onto the belief and grew my faith, I was certain I would find everything that I knew I deserved one day. I just knew I couldn't give up, not yet.

Years went by and I learned who I was and what I truly wanted in life, for the first time ever. After years of self-realization, I healed my heart and learned to love again. It was at this time that I found a bit of myself that I never knew was there. I knew it was going to be a long road, but as I dug down, I saw glimpses of a girl I really liked, and I was excited to get to know her.

Several years later I met the man of my dreams. Finally, when I found the right one, it was easy. I learned I could be the real me that I had just uncovered. I could be raw and transparent and use my voice to express what my needs were. For the first time in my entire life, I was free to be me because I finally knew who I was.

We were engaged 11 months later and married 4 months after that.

As I look back now, I realize that our relationship happened so naturally and easily because we both had the freedom to be ourselves. This allowed us to authentically be the best versions of ourselves.

Chapter Seven: Returning to The Place I Call Home

Life has moved through the years and my husband and I now have two beautiful young daughters.

As fate would have it, we are remodeling the house I grew up in; the same childhood home that I moved out of 20 years ago, and the one where I fell to my knees on the worst day of my life.

When I returned to that same house, that same town, one thing was certain - I was not the same girl. My journey over the last few decades has reminded me that life changes, oftentimes when we're not ready for it.

As I look at the life that I have built today, I feel extreme gratitude that I was able to overcome the hardest days of my life. That I had the strength to keep on fighting, even when at my lowest point, I thought I couldn't. While the road was bumpy and filled with twists and turns, I realize now that it was all part of the greater plan.

If I had given up, I wouldn't have this amazing life that I am living today.

As I look down the driveway holding hands with my husband and daughters, staring at our new dream house, I know I am where I belong, right back to this place that I call home.

THE END.

Cindy M. Taylor

Cindy M. Taylor grew up on a farm in a small country town in Wisconsin. She moved to San Diego shortly after high school where she attributes most of her transformational growth. After going through a divorce, Cindy moved back to the same little town in Wisconsin. She later went on to meet her current husband, with whom she has two beautiful daughters with. As fate would have it, today Cindy and her family are building their dream home on her childhood homestead.

Through the years, she's had a career in sales, marketing and business development, but in her heart, she knows she is meant to be a creator so that she can make an even greater impact in the world.

Cindy is passionate about writing and creating digital courses and products, all in an effort to inspire people to live their best lives. Her mission is to create a legacy so that her daughters and every girl behind her knows that they can achieve their wildest, most audacious dreams and to never, ever give up on what's in their hearts. When Cindy isn't working or writing, she can be found relaxing at her cabin in the North Woods with her family. They enjoy hiking, swimming and the adventures of nature.

Connect with Cindy at www.cindymtaylor.com.

CHAPTER 6

Never Give Up

Ewa Krempa

Be like a postage stamp. Stick to it until you get there.
~ Bob Proctor

Over the years, I rarely shared stories from my youth, as for the most part, they brought back too many memories and feelings. It was easier to suppress them. They have, however, become valuable lessons for me, over the years.

In 1993, when my parents decided to move to Canada, it was an exciting and yet very unfamiliar territory for a young teenager. Growing up in a small village, I did not know much about other places, cultures, and ways of life. Though at school, we studied about the world and such, reading about it and experiencing it were totally different realities. A new country, big city, knowing not a word of English, no friends and missing family back home had left me emotionally broken.

As life continued to show me more contrast, the first five years following the move were the most challenging times for me in many areas of my life.

Signs on giving up on life

If you want to live a happy life, tie it to a goal, not to people or things. ~ Albert Einstein

I knew I was slipping, as I was not passionate about life and withdrew from most family and friends, pretending that things were ok. Perhaps, I felt that I did not want to bother anyone, maybe I did not want to be judged, or I was scared of more criticism. I'd begun to feel overwhelmed by life, instead of excited about it. Negative thoughts filled my subconscious mind. As a teen I was still very active, taking karate lessons, playing for years in the all-city best orchestra, winning art awards, swimming, skating, biking, etc. But inside, I carried a lot of emotional pain.

I am not able to pinpoint the exact year, but in my junior high school years, I faced some of the lowest moments. I remember on a few occasions the self-inflicted wounds and suicidal thoughts.

It can be hard to understand why people harm themselves or want to end their lives. For me it was, perhaps, a way to try to cope with the pain of strong emotions, intense pressure, longing, alienation, and rejection, just to name a few. I was dealing with feelings that seemed too difficult to bear or circumstances I thought I could not change, and I did not know a better way to get rid of the emotional pain.

At a younger age, people who self-harm or have suicidal thoughts may not have yet developed ways to cope, and that was me. My coping skills may have been overpowered by emotions that were too intense. When emotions do not get expressed in a healthy way, tension can build up, sometimes to a point where it seems almost unbearable to continue life. Self-injury, or the attempt to end it all, was a way to release that tension. At least that's what I believed at that time.

Was it the best way? By all means, NO!

There are many ways to cope with difficulties, even big problems, and terrible emotional pain. The help of a mental health professional might be needed for major life troubles or overwhelming emotions. My parents tried to get me help. I remember being on antidepressants for some time, but I eventually refused to continue to take them.

I felt like I was going through things on my own and I wanted to end it all. I couldn't do it, as it turns out, I suppose it was not my time to go. A few years passed, I was exhausted from the emotional rollercoaster and other challenges in my life.

Over the years, the lack of awareness of my true relationship with the infinite power had left me with a distorted image of myself. I was invisible to myself. For years, my thoughts were fueled by ghosts of anger and fear, with a lack of self-confidence and self-love playing on auto pilot in the back of my mind. I can say that I entertained opposing and contradictory ideas for far too long. A lot of my mental activities have led to my stress, exhaustion and failing health. I felt part of my identity fading away. I wanted to be happy again, to live in joy and have a zest for life.

My turning point

> *Life has got all those twists and turns. You've got to hold on tight and off you go.* ~ Nicole Kidman

In my own way and to the best of my ability, I began to take baby steps to adjust to the life around me. It was not easy, as personal development was not something that I was very familiar with at that time. I had to re-educate my mind and make it into a power- producing plant.

I had to let go of who I was, so I could transform into the person I was becoming.

The internal and external rebuilding of my life was under way - it was as if life was dramatically cheering me on with the loudest, clearest physical evidence of breakthroughs.

Fast forward a few years, my entire world was transforming before my eyes, from a past of chaos and stress, hopelessness, and despair, into a life of fulfillment. Each day has become a day filled with new blessings. The impossible became possible when I let go and allowed life to support me.

I'm grateful that I trusted my inner guidance, because I was subsequently blessed with countless miracles that manifested and continue to bless my family and myself today.

In my personal search for a new way of life, I must say, I have been the most difficult person with whom I have ever worked. In fact, I have successfully crossed over the bridge of survival from self inflicted drama to most of my dreams coming true. I believe my personality has taken on a positive character, so that I no longer repel success, but on the contrary, draw it to me. I have left behind me a world of troubles where I felt pushed by life, and I am now living the life of my dreams where I feel empowered. I'm amazed at the way in which things now flow towards me rather than away from me.

As a result, I now help people break through their challenges and transform their lives.

Find something good in everything

Turn your wounds into wisdom. ~ Oprah Winfrey

When you feel like quitting, it takes work to build your inner strength and overcome hardships, but always remember, success and failure are not overnight experiences. It's the small decisions along the way that cause people to fail or succeed. If you can spot the signs of giving up on life, change the path you're on and start achieving again. The power is yours, and

I understand that very well now. Life is constantly changing. That is the nature of life. Sometimes, things happen that are outside of your control. No matter what is going on, you can think. And that is huge.

No matter how much things change, do not let LIFE come to a halt. Choose to keep growing.

Instead of giving up on your goals and dreams, double down. Make sure you stay on track or even get ahead on your goals. If necessary, create new goals that consider the changes that may lie ahead.

There's tremendous power in seeing the good in everything. Sometimes it can be tough to see the good in things. But if you practice pausing, before you respond, you will be able to find something good in any situation, even if it seems really small.

> *In every situation, between the situation and the way we respond to it, there's a space. Start training your mind to use that space to think of something good automatically.* ~ Victor Frankl, Man's Search for Meaning

I practice that technique often now, and it is amazing.

I believe these temporary setbacks are part of life and we must experience them in order to ever be truly successful. Failing at some things on our way to success humbles us and teaches us lessons we need to learn. For people who never give up, failure is simply the fuel for greater determination and success in the future.

Persistence and determination pays off.

> *A little more persistence, a little more effort, and what seemed hopeless failure may turn to glorious <u>success</u>.* ~ <u>Elbert Hubbard</u>

I'll share with you a short story of persistence and determination. While spending some time in Central Europe in 2001, and with money running out fast, I was looking to find work. I decided to try my luck in southern Italy. A lot of people at that time used to leave their loved ones and work aboard to be able to provide for their families. After a long bus ride, arriving at the destination turned out to be quite different than promised. Abandoned in the middle of nowhere, a group of us set up our tents and waited, and waited, for someone to come and take us to work.

Many days passed, a few people from the group had given up waiting and scattered, looking for other opportunities. I had nowhere to go and it would have been disappointing, going back to my family, telling them about what happened. Plus, I hardly had any money left to my name.

Living in a tent under a big old tree for a few days, and walking a few kilometers just to get some bread and water from the nearby town, seemed to take forever. Finally, some Italian guy showed up in a minivan and we all loaded up like little sardines, with all our belongings, to be taken to his work villa.

Weeks went by, working hard in the fields in the scorching sun, collecting crops and making very little pay, it was time to move on. With the help of the local authorities, I found myself, weeks later, at one of the jobs that finally enabled me to save enough money to return to Canada. I could not ask my parents for help, as they were not too pleased with my European adventure. The seasonal job I was able to find at the restaurant by the beach did a lot of good, healing and helping me to reflect. It was definitely one of the best and most enjoyable jobs I have had in my life. I learned Italian very fast, almost fluently within six months, which helped me find that job. Cooking and preparing the meals with an Italian chef was very fulfilling and I learned a lot. I enjoyed my free days by the beach and I remember taking little boat rides to a nearby

Island – Isole Tremiti, a small archipelago in Italy's Adriatic Sea. A day filled with sightseeing, meeting a nice girl from Japan, and just enjoying the blue sea all around. There were a lot of great moments in Italy through out my stay, visiting beautiful towns, eating some of the best ice cream and pizza, meeting some great people, but eventually it was time to return to Canada. It was definitely a learning experience, hard work, but with persistence, I made the best of my time and within a year I was back in Canada.

> *If you make your internal life a priority, then*
> *everything else you need on the outside will be given*
> *to you and it will be extremely clear what the next*
> *step is.* ~ Gabrielle Bernstein

Experiencing multiple breakthroughs throughout my life, elevated me to a new awareness.

The essence of the secret lies in a change of mental attitude. One must learn to live on a different thought basis, and even though change of thinking requires effort, it is much easier than to continue living as you are. The life of strain is difficult. The life of inner peace, being harmonious and without stress, is the easiest type of existence. When I was introduced to personal development, with a combination of programs and reading, I began to see myself doing much more than I hoped for. I began to understand how the mind works and unlocked greater potential in myself.

One of the primary reasons people give up is that they try things, don't succeed, and feel like a failure. The truth is that we are never a failure, unless we give up. When we don't succeed at something, many times, we do not have the courage to try again, and we settle for less than we could achieve or enjoy if we would simply keep trying. The fact is, we all have times when things just don't work out the way we hope they will, even though we do our best. We may fail at one thing, or even a few things, but that certainly does not make us a failure in life.

Another thing worth mentioning, to build up feelings of self-confidence, the practice of suggesting confidence concepts to your mind is very effective. If your mind is obsessed by thoughts of insecurity and inadequacy it is, of course, due to the fact that such ideas have dominated your thinking over a long period of time. Another and more positive pattern of ideas must be given to the mind, and that is accomplished by repetitive suggestion or confidence ideas.

I want you to know there is always a way. It may not be easy; it may not be convenient; it may not come quickly. You may have to go over, under, around, or through. But, if you will simply keep on keeping on and refuse to give up, you will find a way. I went from a life that was happening to me, to one I oversaw and actively designed, and you can too. I believe we are all born with brilliance inside of us. While it seems like it took a while to tap into it, I feel it was necessary, the way it unfolded, so I would have compassion for those going through what I went through, and more.

Living in alignment with my purpose

You are never too old to set another goal or to dream a new dream. ~ Malala Yousafzai

I invite each of you reading this to consider the hidden power of your mindset. All my results were the consequence of my mindset. When I set out to rebuild my life, I did not start with how. I started by looking inward and wondered, "What would I love?" I thought about what needed to be left in place, let go of, or learned anew.

I went through a great amount of inner healing and much of my sickness has dissolved. Best of all, my ability to communicate with others has improved dramatically, and I now connect with people around the world with joy and excitement.

Having transformed my own inner and outer worlds, I know I can help you do the same.

The negative concepts you might be holding in your mind are obstructing the flow of energy which could, if it were given a chance to, breathe new life into you and into your results in life. Step out of your current comfort zone and give yourself permission to live a life that makes you feel excited to get out of bed every morning. When you retake control of yourself and change yourself from within, you can exude the change in your immediate environment. Finally, you are powerful beyond measure with the capacity to make everlasting change that begins with you.

Amazing people showed up in my life and I joined mastermind groups to support me on my journey to what was possible. Find your people, explore a mastermind group, and begin your journey to a future that is worthy of who you are.

I now proudly host a Book Study Club, coach, and mentor people from all over. I have created my own programs to teach and share my knowledge. The act of serving and focusing on others is the most rewarding I've encountered.

All of us have a story to tell, some deeper than others, but all equally important to the universe.

Whatever happens in your life ... Never Give Up!

Ewa Krempa

Ewa Krempa currently resides in Alberta, Canada.

She loves to travel and explore the world and has been to over 50 countries. Her life is full of colourful experiences, memories, and personal growth.

In her leisure time, Ewa loves to spend time in nature, by the ocean, reading & expanding her awareness while raising her daughter and running her businesses.

While she had an interesting life, and some setbacks, she also has many hidden talents and abilities that she has not unleashed. A new mindset of moving forward was truly the catalyst that enabled her to experience and create the world she dreamed of and helps her clients to do the same.

Ewa is a devoted follower of Bob Proctor and Tony Robbins & was privileged to meet Dr. Michael B. Beckwith, Dr. Wayne Dyer and Doreen Virtue where she was inspired by their teachings. A Dr. W. Dyer quote has remained with her thru the years, "If you change the way you look at things, the things you look at change."

Now, Ewa is a founder & CEO of Dynamic Mindset Coaching, where she helps to mentor, coach & transform peoples' lives.

Ewa is one of the authors in Midlife Awakening, where 20 women share inspiring stories of Midlife Transformation. She hosts a weekly Book Study Club, other events & has created her own personal and business development programs. She loves seeing people become better versions of themselves mentally, physically, spiritually, financially, emotionally, and more.

Connect with Ewa at https://linktr.ee/EwaKrempa.

CHAPTER 7

Life Can Change in a Split Second

Jacalyn Price

There is always a choice. Challenges are a part of life; some are small and some much larger. Sometimes, the smallest challenge can be a breaking point. It's how you deal with those challenges that you learn from and become stronger for it.

Even from a young age, you are faced with challenges. For example, when you first learn to ride a push bike, you fall off and get back on it. Improve your skills. There will always be challenges, from when you start primary school, to secondary school, then from studying at TAFE - Technical and Further Education or university or a career you have chosen, your first place of employment. You may encounter health challenges that affect your life or your family. It's important you don't try and resolve them by yourself, there is always help out there. Once you talk to people, you will find out others have faced the same or similar challenges.

In this chapter, I'm sharing the challenges I have faced and how I dealt with and overcame them using the power of the subconscious mind. You can overcome any challenge you may come across, as well.

No matter what challenges you face, you have a choice to either stay where you are OR be determined to stay strong, overcome them and move on. It's your choice. Always have VISION. Like Helen Keller, she had no sight, but she had VISION. A lot of people have sight, but no VISION and are missing out on a lot in their life. Many people think on their death bed … if only. Live each day as if it is your last, as tomorrow is never promised.

THE CLOCK OF LIFE
The clock of life is wound but once,
    And no man has the power,
    To tell just when the hands will stop,
    At late or early hour.

To lose one's wealth is sad indeed,
    To lose one's health is more,
    To lose one's soul is such a loss
    That no man can restore.

The present only is our own,
    So live, love, toil with a will,
    Place no faith in "Tomorrow,"
    For the Clock may then be still.
    — Robert H. Smith

Many famous people have overcome many challenges, from childhood, in business and in life and found a way to overcome them.

Always say yes to the opportunity.
~ Sir Richard Branson
Change your story, change your life. ~ Tony Robbins

I have a dream. ~ Martin Luther King
Be the change you want to see in the world.
~ Mahatma Gandhi
Everything is energy. ~ Albert Einstein

This is my story

My name is Jacalyn Price. I see, hear, feel, and know that my purpose in life is to touch hearts and change one person at a time. When I completed high school at 18 years old, I wanted to join the police force and work in forensics. However, I didn't meet the requirements, a female had to be 24 years old, and be five foot six inches in height. I was too short and too young. I was prepared, I had trained and was very fit.

When one door closes, another opens.
~ Alexander Graham Bell

So, I decided to study as a Pathology Technician and worked at the Royal Newcastle Hospital. This involved going to college for four years, while I worked. Once I met the age requirement of 24, I was still too short, they didn't drop the height limit until I was 32 years old. Then I was too old. Things have changed a lot since then. I continued my career in Newcastle, at the hospital and after the earthquake in 1989, they relocated us to the John Hunter Hospital at New Lambton. I worked in pathology, as a laboratory technician for over 25 years. I was fit, healthy, and loved my life.

A simple fall at work

One day my entire work dynamic changed. I had what was initially a simple fall. I felt embarrassed, and then continued my day at work. But, within two hours, I had intense burning pain, in my left hip. I struggled to drive home from work. I didn't sleep very well that night and called in sick the next day.

I visited my local GP; he sent me for x-rays, and nothing showed up. The pain was so intense that I had a couple of days off and then returned to work. Pain relief wasn't helping much. I had to have more time off work. They decided to reduce my work hours to four hours a day to see if I could manage, this wasn't working either. My pain would increase as the day went on.

I went back to my GP. They did an MRI, and again nothing showed up. Then work decided I could work two hours a day at another location. It meant driving longer to do two hours' work. No one believes you're in pain if it doesn't show up on any test.

Then overnight, my left leg went completely numb. I thought I had a stroke; the pain was intense. My leg felt cold and was bright pink. I went by ambulance to a Toronto private hospital. The specialist, Dr. Pacey, diagnosed my medical problem. Reflex Sympathetic Dystrophy or chronic regional pain syndrome. The sympathetic nervous system was affected. I was seen by nerve specialists and taken to the hydrotherapy pool twice a day to try and get movement in my leg.

After a month, I started to get some feeling and slowly my left leg had more feeling. The pain was still there and sensitive to touch. I couldn't even tolerate having any clothing on my leg. Due to the swelling, even shoes were a problem and I had to wear a larger size.

Once I got home, I needed help in the shower. I had the bathroom modified to a walk-in shower, because I couldn't lift my left leg into the tub. I couldn't stand a towel on my leg even, so I used a hairdryer to dry it off. I had a ramp put at the front of the house for wheelchair access and a verandah put around the house. I used the wheelchair in the house, and needed help with cooking, and all basic needs.

I went to physio three times weekly by hired car. They used a lift to put me into the hydro pool. The physio would try to massage my leg, but it was so painful. Slowly, but surely, she was able to touch my left leg and moisturize it gently.

My life revolved around hydro and physio and pain management clinics. I joined a group of people who also suffered with RSD. Some had different limbs affected, and they don't tell you it can spread to other areas of your body. Mine did, as did many others.

There is no cure, sometimes in young people it burns itself out. Over time, it can go into remission, but can return with a simple injury. Mine did many years later. There was a choice to cut the nerve, but the risk was great, and I was still quite young. I had nerve blocks in my left hip, you are in theatre and can watch as they put a needle into your hip, locate the area, then are injected. It was a weird feeling. Guanethidine block was inserted in my left foot. A high pressure torniquet was placed on my leg. I could not stand the pain, so they put me to sleep.

I had lots of pain relief, and a number of ketamine infusions in the rehab hospital. They start a low dose and increase the dose and then decrease it over a period of time. One time I woke up as if I were drunk, the doctor called in and laughed. She said we had better lower the dose. With strong pain relief you can't function properly, are always sleepy, and can't think clearly. In the rehab clinics, we went to meditation classes to try and relax and breathe through the pain. Nerve pain is the worst pain. I had a frame in my bed for the blankets, as I could not stand anything on my left leg.

The neurologist said I had to try and use my left leg. If you don't use it, you lose it. After the nerve blocks, I was able to slowly bear weight on my left leg. While in a wheelchair most of the time, even when shopping. I started using Canadian crutches. And I was using a four-wheeled walking frame. With brackets, I was able to attach the crutches to the walking frame. Slowly but surely, I could put some more weight on my left leg. It was weak compared to the right leg.

I was able to purchase a car with a mobility scooter in the back that had a crane to lift it out. Once I could drive, I could then go to the shops and use the mobility scooter to get around.

My hydro, physio, and pain management clinics continued. I started using my crutches even more in the house to strengthen my left leg and over time was able to get stronger. I learnt new techniques to help with the pain, tapping, meditation, chakra therapy and using the power of the subconscious mind. I was able to greatly reduce my pain medication.

After 13 years of wheelchairs, mobility scooters, walking frames and crutches, I was able to manage without them. I still kept the crutches in the car for 12 months, just in case, then decided it was time to let go.

When I decided to return to work in pathology, I was told I had been out of work too long, that they preferred younger staff. So, I decided to look for another way. I started doing courses in business skills and I worked with a coach. I had been out of work for so long, I had to think differently. It was difficult at first. I was determined to learn more. I read personal development books. Listened to inspiring people like Zig Ziglar and Jim Rohn.

One of the courses was with Paul Blackburn, called the mindset riddle. This led me on a trip to Thailand where we had a wonderful experience in our classes. We had the Monks join us and bless us. Then on the beach, we lit lanterns and released them into the sky. Imagine all those lanterns floating skyward. Picture perfect.

What you think, you become

I started working, in my local area, as an Avon representative going door to door meeting a lot of people. It was a rewarding experience, looking after other people's needs with products to use for themselves, their families, and friends. I worked for them for seven years until Avon ceased in Australia, a shock for all concerned. Avon had been in existence for over 50 years in Australia and a lot longer worldwide. You don't realize how many lonely people are out there who often have no one to talk to. My Aunt Eve and my mum would assist me with packing orders and my Aunt Eve would help me with deliveries. I was in the top 50 in Australia in sales. This led me to win a seven-night cruise around the islands of Queensland and I won the Mrs. Albee award. I continued with my studies, learning and teaching, as Jim Rohn would say.

My next adventure

I then started learning with Tony Robbins, going to live events and zoom events, Date with Destiny, and Business Mastery. At the Sydney event, Unleash the Power Within, I along with hundreds of others did the fire walk. Using the power of the subconscious mind, Tony prepares you to walk over hot coals imagining them as cool moss. I am unstoppable.

I was then introduced to a networking business opportunity with ACN, All Communications Network. I joined business groups, made a lot of new business connections, made a lot of new friends, and attended business meetings both local and national.

After joining a business networking group, I was encouraged to enter a business award. I entered the Bx Business Awards, made the finals, and was announced Business of the Year in 2020 and 2021 with Bx Business networking for ACN for Business services. I also have articles published in the Bx xClusive magazine.

I then entered other business awards. I have made the finals with Hunter Region Business Excellence Awards, Australian Small Business Champions awards, Australian Women's Small Business Champions Awards, Local Business Awards,

Australian Ladies in Business Initiative Awards and Bx Business xCellence Awards.

I was ecstatic making the finals, attending red carpet events at two of the finals, at the star event centre in Sydney. First class entertainment, delicious three course meals and meeting over 1000 finalists, making new connections, and getting dressed up in formal wear, it was amazing. Other finalists were in different locations, all exclusive, delicious meals, and meeting other finalists.

While doing a course with Matt Morris, I was asked if I would like to co-author with him. I said YES!

> *Say Yes to the opportunity. They work out how*
> *to do it.* ~ Richard Branson

My book is called, *Breakthrough Leadership with Jacalyn Price.* I'm chapter one. There are 29 other leading experts in this book.

When I was younger, I had often thought about authoring a book, being able to share my experiences in life. We go through so many changes, challenges, and learn new things while living our lives. It's not until you are asked to share, that a lot of memories come back. I'm grateful for all the things I have experienced in life, and I am always learning, every day you learn something new. I love to share my experiences with others.

While visiting Dad in hospital, there was a lady opposite him in a lot of pain. I went to her. She was waiting for a hip replacement and had to wait five months. I talked a while, gave her ideas on how to control the pain, saying positive thoughts. She was trying to get into bed, and said, "I can't turn," I said, "Yes, you can." She kept saying it over and over, "Yes I can," and then smiled when she did. We talked a while longer; I gave her more tips on controlling her pain using the power of the subconscious mind. We are now going to stay connected. She is one happier lady.

I am now in collaboration with three more books by simply joining an author's group with Lynda Sunshine West and Sally Green. Listening and attending training and saying, "YES" to the opportunity. There are also opportunities for more collaboration books and in time, my own book. I had always dreamed of writing a book, sharing my story, my experiences, sharing what I learn from my mentors and coaches. I have an article in the Newcastle Weekly Magazine as a finalist in the Hunter Region Business Excellence Awards highlighting my ACN business. I am doing a course with Peter Sage Elite Membership Forum, and when finished I will be a trainer, helping others, sharing what Peter has taught me.

Age is not a barrier; you never stop learning. I'm doing more now than I was doing 20 years go.

She believed she could, so she did. ~ R.S. Grey

The best things in life are the people you love, the places you've been, and the memories you've made along the way. Live every moment. Laugh every day. Love beyond words.

Happiness is something you decide on ahead of time. It's a decision I make every morning when I wake up - I have a choice. Each day is a gift, as long as I have my eyes open, I'll focus on the new day and all the happy memories I've stored away, just for this time in my life. Old age is like a bank account you withdraw from what you've put in. So deposit a lot of happiness in the bank account of memories.

5 simple rules to be happy
1. Free your heart from hatred.
2. Free your mind from worries.
3. Live simply.
4. Give more.
5. Expect less and enjoy every moment.

I have a powerful WHY. Have a WHY that wakes you up every morning excited for the day. Your WHY changes over time, depending on the circumstances and challenges you face. My WHY is to set up a foundation for people with illness, making it possible for them to access funding for medications and treatments. After my sister, Jen, developed breast cancer and had to pay a large sum for radiation treatment. Finding your WHY is like having a lighthouse to guide you towards fulfillment.

Always remember to dress for success. No matter where you go. To business meetings or when you're out and about. You want to make an impression. First impressions count. Be the light when you walk into a room. Smile and be confident and ready to make a difference. Smiling is contagious. Change your story. Change your life. If I can do it, so can you.

What you think, you become. And remember to NEVER GIVE UP. My favourite song is I AM WOMAN by Helen Reddy. I AM STRONG. I AM INVINCIBLE. I AM WOMAN. The choice to NEVER GIVE UP will make you and you will become stronger by overcoming the challenges you face, no matter how big or small, using the power of the subconscious mind. and living the best life you deserve.

I am Jacalyn Price, Author, Entrepreneur, Speaker, Business Owner, and Investor.

I am a dream maker, touching hearts and changing lives one person at a time.

Jacalyn Price

Jacalyn Price won Business of the Year in Business Services for ACN in 2020, 2021. She has articles published in the Bx xClusive magazine. She belongs to the following networking groups: Business at breakfast, Edward Zia networking community, Lake Macquarie Women in Business, More Marketing Ideas, Bconnected World, Happy Neighborhood Project. She has been a host and speaker at her networking events. A finalist in Hunter Region Business Excellence Awards, Australian Small Business Champions Awards, Australian Women's Small Business Champions Awards, Local Business Awards, Australian Ladies in Business Initiative Awards, Bx Business xCellence Awards. Jacalyn has an article in the Newcastle Weekly, highlighting her ACN Business.

Jacalyn's key to success is personal development. Some of her biggest influences are Bob Proctor, Zig Ziglar, Mary Morrisey, Jim Rohn, Tony Robbins, Grant Cardone, Simon Sinek, and Peter Sage to name a few.

Her life mission is to set up a foundation for people with illness to access funding for medication and treatments. This was after her sister, Jen, was diagnosed with Breast Cancer and had to pay a large sum for radiation treatment. Jacalyn loves taking the burdens off families. Touching Hearts and Changing Lives.

Every day for her is a new day, new thoughts, strengths, and possibilities.

Connect with Jacalyn at www.jacalynp.acnibo.com.

CHAPTER 8

Never, Never, Never, Never Give Up

Jeff Mudd

I can still recall my middle school history teacher telling us about the famous *Never Give In* address delivered by Winston Churchill.

My teacher wasn't much interested in the historical accuracy of the moment because what he told us was a bit closer to legend or myth than fact. Essentially, we were taught that one day Winston Churchill, the esteemed prime minister of Great Britain, was brought to the podium to inspire and encourage his audience with a stirring speech.

As my teacher told it, Churchill strolled to the microphone, let the crowd sit in uncomfortable silence, and then with passion and conviction delivered a six-word speech: "Never, never, never, never give up." And then he sat down, and the people cheered wildly, and they won the war.

Like I said, my teacher's lecture was missing some details, but most of us were thrilled to walk away having learned a few important lessons:

1. You could draft a six-word essay for your next assignment and claim it was great.

2. You can get pretty far in life even with a very limited vocabulary.

3. You should never ever give up on anything.

As far as that educational experience is concerned, only the third lesson was worth anything.

Later in life, I decided to learn more about this historical moment because, quite frankly, the story my teacher told seemed incomplete.

Here's what I would uncover:

On October 29th, 1941, Winston Churchill appeared at the Harrow School in London. He'd been invited to speak to the faculty and the student body on the topic of perseverance and courage in the face of adversity.

Not much has been said about the entire speech, but what has become famous and has lived on in the middle school classrooms of America is this portion of the speech:

> *Never give in. Never give in. Never, never, never,*
> *never—in nothing, great or small, large, or petty—*
> *never give in, except to convictions of honor and*
> *good sense. Never yield to force; never yield to the*
> *apparently overwhelming might of the enemy.*
> ~Winston Churchill

At the time of his speech, the eventual outcome of the war was uncertain, and Great Britain was in jeopardy. In fact, it was a critical time for the entire world, and those in attendance were desperate to hear something positive, to hear some information that might give them hope of victory and a quick resolution of the terrible war.

Churchill didn't predict an end to the war or proclaim victory, and he didn't just provide some vague and complex word salad as politicians typically do.

Instead, Churchill provided his audience with a way of living. He shared with them a simple, straightforward strategy not only for winning a war but also for winning at life.

Because the speech was broadcast over the radio, millions of people around the world heard it, and it would become one of the most famous speeches in modern history. So famous that my teacher would share it with me and my classmates many years later—although, without much precision.

How To Not Give Up

I think we can agree that it's ok for a 12-year-old to think a country was inspired to win a war by a six-word speech, but what's missing from the lesson is how Churchill put that *Never Give In* slogan into practice.

Just being stubborn or refusing to change your mind will not lead to success. There's an approach to winning at life (or a war) that goes beyond persevering through difficulty.

Don't get me wrong ... that's vital, but it's not enough.

Allow me to share an analogy that might help. Imagine your daughter is playing in the yard and tosses her favorite doll into the air, but it does not come back down. It's lodged in the gutter that runs along the roof of your home. She comes into the house crying, and you're about to play the role of the hero and retrieve the toy.

So, you start to jump as high as you can, throwing yourself against the side of the house until you break your ankle.

In the above scenario, your refusal to give up on getting that doll might be admirable, but it's also stupid. When you lack a plan or a strategy, refusing to give up is just obstinance. Imagine how much better this process would go if you just asked your neighbor for his step ladder.

In this scenario, each step of that ladder is a part of your process. Each rung is a smaller, tactically placed goal that takes you closer to your final target in measured stages.

You see, one essential element in not giving up is setting clear goals which will work as steps. These steps are invaluable not only because they require some forethought and planning but also because they provide you with immediate information about how you're doing. They tell you if you're achieving what you set out to do. What brings these steps to life is placing a timeline or completion dates for each step, otherwise you can put off each goal or task without any personal accountability.

For Churchill, the target was winning the war, but he needed a plan. As Prime Minister, Churchill established several key strategies to win the war:

First, he focused his attention on Nazi Germany. There were other enemies in the Axis powers, but Churchill knew Germany was the linchpin. If Hitler could be toppled, his allies would fall apart.

Second, Churchill knew he needed the United States in his corner. A strong relationship with the United States was essential to his success.

Another goal Churchill set was to maintain the support of British citizens, which is why he gave his famous speech (along with many others). He needed the people he represented to commit to his plan with the same dedication and perseverance that he showed.

Additionally, Churchill focused his attention on securing North Africa. He saw that region of the world as vital to allow his forces (and his allies forces) access to invade Europe.

Finally, Great Britain began developing innovative military technologies. Specifically, they sought to build new equipment, implement new tactics, and design better weapons.

The point is you can't just achieve something great by determining you will and then never giving up. Banging your head into a wall over and over again might eventually break it down, but you won't be around to see it.

You need a plan, and you need to establish goals along with a timeline, which will lead to the completion of that plan.

The Benefits of Goal Setting

There are several benefits to creating steps toward a final goal beyond just reaching the destination:

1. Goals provide direction and focus. There are countless ways to get from the East Coast to the West Coast, but some of them are much easier than others. Establish a path before taking that first step.

2. Goals increase motivation and build momentum. An NFL team only wins the Superbowl after winning enough of the first 17 games to qualify for additional games. Then it needs to win the divisional round. Then the conference round. Along the way, the team is becoming more and more dedicated to winning the Super Bowl - they are thriving on the momentum they've built, their belief and investment in the dream is increasing with each smaller success.

3. Goals are measurable and keep us accountable. If you have any second thoughts, doubts, or worries, looking back on your accomplishments can be encouraging. When you're halfway up that ladder and the doll on the roof still seems far away, look down and count how many steps you've taken. There's measurable proof of your success.

4. Goals provide clarity. Most journeys toward success are complicated and difficult - otherwise, why would we need inspiration to not give up? Having clearly defined goals allows you to recalibrate and it gives you an opportunity to communicate with others who might be able to help along the way.

5. Goals build resilience. Similar to the benefits shared in #2, your smaller victories build muscle. You're getting

stronger, wiser, better. You're adapting and evolving with each step, and the farther you get along the way to your dream, the more likely you'll be to stick with it. You're building resolve and that tough skin.

Overall, setting clear goals leads to success in both your personal and professional life because goals provide a clear roadmap for achieving desired outcomes and help you stay focused, motivated, and accountable. Speaking of accountability, one of my mentors, Greg S. Reid, created this quote:

A Dream Written Down with Dates Becomes a Goal!
A Goal Broken down into Steps Becomes a Plan! A
Plan backed by Action Makes Your Dreams come
True! ~Greg S. Reid

Let's cover some steps to <u>Never Give-Up</u>!

1. Goals that are worth completing can be hard, sometimes you get hit with challenges that require you to take a step back or a short break. Make a decision to take a break or redirect your effort or time off. But set a get back on track time also.

    Winners Never Quit and quitters never win
    ~Vince Lombardi

2. Attitude can be a killer of dreams and a force to push you thru challenges. Control your attitude by being positive. Surround yourself with positive, resilient, supportive people who will help you, hold you accountable for your goals.

3. Habits and Routines are keyways to completing each step of your goal. When you have a daily routine of working on the steps you have laid out each day or a

set time every weekend for the extra effort outside of your job. Each day, each weekend of time commitment adds up over the long term. Stay focused on your goal by having a routine that adds up to a winning habit.

4. Remember the *Why*. Knowing why your goal is important to you is key. Why is a great motivator feeding your brain and soul with the energy you need to push through Not Giving up. Feed yourself with motivational materials, but they will not work without you being responsible and the main motivator for your goals.

Never giving up is a phrase that has been used in many contexts and situations to encourage individuals to persevere through challenging times. It means that despite the difficulties, setbacks, and obstacles encountered, one should not quit or abandon one's goals, dreams, or aspirations. It involves displaying resilience, determination, and a willingness to keep moving forward, no matter how tough things may seem. The act of not giving up requires a great deal of mental strength and emotional stability. It means being able to withstand failure and disappointment, and to bounce back from these experiences even stronger. It means being able to confront fear and uncertainty and push past one's comfort zone. It involves having a positive mindset, focusing on the solutions rather than the problems, and using failures and setbacks as opportunities for growth and improvement.

One of the main benefits of never giving up is that it leads to personal growth and development. When an individual does not give up, they develop resilience, perseverance, and determination, which are important traits for success in any area of life. Additionally, the more one perseveres through challenges, the more confident and capable they become, and the more you are able to achieve your goals and aspirations.

Another benefit of never giving up is that it inspires others. When others witness an individual's determination and resilience, they are often motivated to follow suit. This can create a positive ripple effect, as others are encouraged to pursue their own goals and dreams with a similar level of commitment and determination.

However, it is important to note that never giving up does not mean being stubborn or inflexible. It means being able to adapt to changing circumstances and learning from mistakes and failures. It also means knowing when to seek help or advice from others who may have more knowledge or experience in a particular area.

In conclusion, never giving up is a powerful mindset that can lead to personal growth, success, and inspiration for others. It involves being resilient, determined, and adaptable in the face of challenges and setbacks. By embodying this mindset, individuals can achieve their goals and aspirations, and inspire others to do the same.

Jeff Mudd

Jeff Mudd is the founder of the Best Rate Repair Company. With over three decades of experience in the construction industry, Jeff has established himself as an expert in the field of wood rot repair, termite damage repair, and general construction.

Jeff's interest in the construction industry began at a young age. He honed his skills working with a few termite companies in San Diego, then as a termite inspector for several years, before starting his own company.

In 2002, Jeff founded Best Rate Repair Company, a San Diego-based company specializing in wood rot and termite damage repair. The company gained a reputation for quality workmanship and excellent customer service, earning Jeff recognition in the industry.

Jeff has continued to expand the scope of his business, adding services such as deck and fence repair, to meet the changing needs of his customers. Today, Best Rate Repair Company is a thriving business with a new Owner and Management team of skilled professionals who share Jeff's commitment to excellence.

In 2021, Jeff decided to use his expertise to promote the construction trades to young adults. He started *The Trades Podcast,* a Podcast show that aims to educate and inspire young people to pursue careers in the construction industry. Through the podcast, Jeff shares his own experiences and interviews other professionals in the field, providing valuable insights and advice to listeners.

Connect with Jeff at www.thetradespodcast.com.

CHAPTER 9

Successfully Navigating the Choppy Waters of Academe

Kimberly Adams Tufts

n 2018, while serving as the Interim Associate Dean for a College of Health Sciences, I was called to the Dean's office to meet with the Interim Associate Dean & Assistant Dean. I thought "This is great! The Dean is probably going to finally approve my budget for next year. Then I can get on with implementing my plan for a year of faculty capacity building." Yet in my heart I knew this perspective lacked truth. I knew something was wrong, because it was May and my fiscal year budget had yet to be approved. However, I arrived at the meeting in full force Pollyanna mode.

Once I was seated, the interim Dean informed me that I was being removed from my position as Interim Dean, wherein I had served for 18 months. Then the Assistant Dean took over. She said, "We are eliminating your position." You see, she was to assume the permanent Dean position in less than a month. She went on to explain to me that, "You have done such a great job as Assistant & Interim Associate Dean. Therefore, we are turning over your responsibilities to the faculty."

I was stunned! ... My mind was reeling! You see, if I was no longer part of the Dean's Team I would be re-assigned to the School of Nursing (SON). The same SON that I decided to cut ties with four years earlier. In the winter of 2014, I took a new job, in a leadership role, in another State. When I informed the Chair of the SON and the Dean of the College, to retain me, the Dean created a Dean's Team position for me. She appointed me as the inaugural Assistant Dean for Interprofessional Education (IPE). A new position, a new initiative, new responsibilities, with very little resources. This was no problem for me. I was often called *the go-ahead* girl at my previous University. Need someone who's not afraid of challenges, who can effectively communicate a vision, and garner support from others. Get Kimberly!

So, in the Summer of 2014, I took on my new responsibilities with a vengeance. I recruited faculty and other institutions as collaborators. I obtained College and University-wide commitment to IPE. By Spring of 2018, faculty, and administrators from four external Colleges and Universities had collaborated to advance IPE. We had an IPE day in March 2018, wherein 400 faculty and students participated. What a heady experience! I had even elicited support from another institution to pay for the food.

Yet, on that Monday after Spring graduation, I was stunned. "It's okay," I thought. "I'll take the summer to put some things in place, to do some succession planning." I voiced my plan to the Interim Dean and Assistant Dean. I said "I will work with the IPE Advisory Committee over the Summer. We will get the plans in place for the First Year Student IPE Orientation Day." They told me, "No that won't work. Your contract is up May 24th." I thought, "Ten days, you are giving me ten days' notice." Ten days, because it was possible, unlike all the others on the Dean's Team, I had been appointed to a 10-month rather than a 12-month contract. My Summer contract was a year-by-year arrangement.

The Assistant Dean then informed me that in the next hour they would be meeting with the Chair of the School of Nursing to give her input regarding my Fall semester assignment. I continued to be stunned. I looked at the Interim Dean with begging eyes. "Please help me," my eyes said, "You know me." "You asked me to take this position to support you. I worked for you when you led the School of Nursing. Don't do this to me." I begged with my eyes.

I left the Dean's suite and walked up to my own corner office, stunned, with tears in my eyes. I called a colleague who was the Dean of another College. I said, "Please come." She said, "I will be right there." She came. I cried, cried, and cried. She asked, "What do you want?" I said, "I want to stay on this campus, rather than be assigned to another campus."

Two weeks later, I met with the University President to seek his help. He heard my story. He reinforced that what I had experienced was unjust. He let me know that he had assumed with the coming of the new Dean, I would be permanently appointed as Associate Dean. He asked what I wanted. That question again. I said, "I just want an office on this campus." He looked at me quizzically. I felt uncomfortable under his gaze. I asked, "What are you thinking, that I advocate for everyone else, but I don't advocate for myself?" He shook his head yes. He was sad. I was even sadder.

You see, not only was I a former Assistant/Associate Dean of a College. I was a tenured full Professor. A rarity for women in academe. Yet, I had no power. Or more truthfully, I thought I didn't have any power. I didn't say I am going to grieve this via the Faculty Senate, or I am going to the Office of Institutional Equity. I just wanted an office.

I didn't get that office. The provost told me he couldn't give me favoritism. I was assigned to the SON in a remote setting, away from the main campus.

I was scared, disappointed, depressed. Hence, when I went to Quebec that summer for a Nursing leadership experience with Caroline Adams Miller, the author of *Getting Grit*. I was subdued, I did not enjoy the city, the food, the people. While I was there, the Graduate Program Director in the SON emailed that I was assigned to teach women's health to graduate students and leadership to undergraduate students. I built my career teaching public policy, health policy, social determinants of health, research methods, and publication. "Women's health?" I thought. I cried.

That Fall, during the dedication of the SON's new space, I was assigned to be a tour guide when the University President and State Governor visited the School of Nursing, rather than a leadership role. When the President whispered, "Are you okay?" as I stood at the top of the stairs in my tour guide role. I smiled through my pain. That very evening, I attended an event where I sat in the front row with the other community leaders as the Governor gave the keynote address at a local hospital celebration. Yet, I was not treated as a leader in my own institution.

It got worse, when students from three institutions came to the campus for the monthly IPE day, I was assigned as a timekeeper to go to the various classrooms with a time warning rather than to share my IPE expertise. My own graduate student was given a more meaningful role.

I thought, "How did I get here?" At that moment, I didn't know. Yet, now I know it was the culmination of years of accepting the unacceptable, not giving voice to my concerns, and/or not seeking external support.

Recruited to a New Institution

In 2004, I was recruited to a School of Nursing in a University in the southeastern part of the United States. I accepted a non-tenured Associate Professor position. I was so excited! I wanted to continue my work as a nursing faculty member while living in a warm sunny climate. Previously, I had been an Associate Professor at one of the top five ranked Schools of Nursing in the world. I was also the first Fellow in the American Academy of Nursing to be faculty at my new school.

It was a bit of an adjustment. The office spaces and buildings were not nearly as comfortable, and I was given an inner office space without windows. Because the campus was located between two rivers in a low-lying area that often flooded, I had to make sure I wore sandals. Notably, two faculty members tried to pay me for their meals the first time I ate in the faculty dining room. I thought, "It's okay I am young looking. I have on a white top with black pants and no one else looks like me in the dining room."

"I didn't care!" I thought, "I am in Virginia. The home of my ancestors and it's constantly sunny. The world is my oyster."

How little I knew ...

Academic Record & Integrity Questioned

Early on I had been told, "Be quiet and keep doing good work. Your great contributions will be recognized, your work will speak for itself."

About four months after arriving at my new school, the new Associate Dean for Research asked for a meeting with me. He told me that he and the Dean were looking to build up the research and scholarship enterprise for the College. He reported that a meeting had taken place with the research and scholarship leaders from each of the five schools in the College. He said, in preparation for the meeting, he had researched the academic records of various faculty members. After doing the research he and the Dean agreed that I would most likely be a good choice to be part of this initiative. However, he said that when he proposed that to the group. The faculty person representing the SON said, that although those citations were on my CV, she didn't think I was the person who wrote the proposals. When the Associate Dean for Research asked me about it, I didn't take offense or get angry. I responded, "Well, they are all public. You can use the grant number to look it up. Also, if I wasn't the lead investigator or program director, I indicated who was in the citation on my CV." I had several millions of dollars of funded projects on my record including National Institutes of Health and Robert Woods Johnson Foundation grant funds. But I didn't question them or stand up for myself. I thought, "I will just keep my head down and continue my research. They will see. I will prove to them that I am a good scholar."

Work Stolen

About ten years later, I felt I had made a place for myself in my new institution. I had served as Director of the new doctoral program, been the faculty lead for a university-wide diversity initiative, been the Director of SON community & global health programming, obtained new funding, served as Treasurer and President of the University Women's Caucus. The list goes on. Because you see, I was always trying to do more, be more, be accepted. Even though my CV was double or triple the size of my colleagues, my credibility was continually questioned by one faculty member. She and I were one of three Associate Professors in the SON. During this period, although I had two different Chairs in the School, neither advocated for me with that faculty member. So, I thought "I just have to do more."

Interprofessional education (IPE) emerged as an education trend for the health professions. I decided to write a grant proposal for an IPE collaborative project among three of the Schools in the College. I went to the heads of two Schools, brought them up to speed on the concept of IPE, and suggested we partner. One of them was excited about the topic and the partnership. The other leader was skeptical. I, therefore, had to do additional research about IPE and write a concept paper about my idea, before she was onboard. In my excitement I told the Chair of the SON. She implied that she thought it was a great idea. She felt the project had great potential for advancing the School of Nursing's scholarship enterprise. She stated that she wanted various faculty to work together to build up the school. She called a meeting, wherein individual faculty presented their scholarship ideas. My concept paper was well received. In the upcoming weeks, a faculty member approached the Chair and said she wanted to write the proposal for the IPE project. The Chair informed me of this. I thought, "Oh, she will never allow her to take my work." Some days later, the Chair entered my office and told me she had decided to allow the other faculty person to write the proposal. She gave me various reasons for coming to this decision.

That night, I was noticeably quiet at home. During dinner, my husband asked me what was going on. I told him what had happened. We had a large rectangular kitchen. My husband got up and began to pace. He seemed quite distressed. I thought, "Oh at least someone understands." He turned around and said, "What's wrong with you that you would allow someone to take your professional opportunity?"

I always believed in the system and thought that I would be asked to be a part of the grant team even if I didn't lead it. I kept thinking my two colleagues would say, "This was all Kimberly's idea," and I would be invited to work on the grant proposal. Spring came and passed. The grant proposal was submitted. Early in Fall semester, I was walking across campus with one of my colleagues. She said, "We got word; we got the grant funding." I was shocked. Because I was now an Assistant Dean of the College, I next went to a meeting of the leaders of the College. The Dean of the College asked the Chair of the SON to, "Share your good news." She announced, "The project has been funded for 1.2 million dollars." I felt sick and excused myself to go to the bathroom. I cried. I told my husband later that if I hadn't been in a public place, I would have screamed out loud.

Became an Over Worker

How did I cope with being looked over, with being told no, too many times to count? I became an over worker. I took on several new initiatives for my School and University. I did what was asked of me and thought of other ways to advance my career. I collaborated with women across campus on research projects. I constantly submitted abstracts and presented them at national and international conferences. I joined a research network outside of the SON, sought funding, and led an interprofessional research team. I mentored doctoral students through their research. I served on numerous committees, taskforces, and professional organizations. I worked hard, weekends and holidays included. My overworking impacted my personal relationships.

I remember being at a party and someone asked what I did for work. I answered, "I teach online." The person said something like, "That must be convenient ... you must have a flexible schedule." Before I could respond, my husband said, with an edge in his voice, "No, she works, she works at night, she works in the morning, she works on the weekend, on vacations." I was standing there in shock. Yet, I knew what he said was true. I knew my overworking was taking a toll on my marriage.

Never Give Up

I have many stories to tell. As a women faculty member, as a woman of color, I have been overlooked, questioned, taken advantage of many times. Yet, the point of my story is to highlight how I coped, overcame, & did not give up!

You see I never thought I was unique. That I was the only one. I am not that special. I also had evidence that others were taken advantage of by the faculty person who questioned my work and who later stole my work. We had a joke. "Be careful what you write in an email. If it's good enough, she will take it."

My turning point was working with a coach. That coach helped me to:

- Create space for thinking/brainstorming
- Have the confidence to ask for what I wanted
- Set boundaries and say no
- Prioritize my work
- Develop systems for redirecting and reenergizing myself

I learned to be strategically productive, not busy. I also made an intentional decision that I would not be driven away. That I would use my experience and lessons to help others.

Traditional advice has it that to move up the academic ranks, you must be a good teacher, an established scholar, and a good University citizen. How? Learn your craft, network with others, participate in collaborative work, serve the University.

What does that look like? I can tell you. I did all of those:

- I learned to be an excellent online teacher. I then shared what I learned by doing presentations, providing resources with others, and mentoring others in teaching-learning.
- I wrote research project proposals. When I got good scores, I shared what I learned with faculty colleagues in my college and beyond.
- I often attended university-wide events to meet others with whom I could potentially work.
- I accepted invitations for collaborative work that resulted in funded work, many publications, and national as well as international presentations and several professional awards.

- When I was awarded funding, I brought on early career faculty and students, providing mentorship, coaching, & training.
- I supported others' development. For example, I started the "Agraphia Group" without seeking permission from Chair of the School or Dean of the College. I helped several early career nursing faculty members to kick off their own scholarship journeys.

So, despite the barriers and obstacles, I never gave up. I intentionally & mindfully put one foot in front of the other. The result was that when I applied for Full Professor, my application received all positive votes at all six levels of approval. The formula works.

It will work for you also. I coach and empower faculty women to create that life and career they really want.

Kimberly Adams Tufts

Kimberly Adams Tufts "Dr. KAT" achieved the rank of full professor in academe. She is also a Fellow in the American Academy of Nursing. She is the current vice-chair for the Academy Expert Panel on Emerging Infectious Diseases. Dr. KAT is a published author with more than 40 publications including articles, books, and abstracts to her credit. She is also an award-winning teacher. Notably, Dr. KAT has received more than 7 million dollars in funding from NIH, HRSA, and various foundations in support of her work. During the COVID-19 pandemic, she served as the Chief of Education, Research, & Development at a Veterans Medical Center.

Her big WHY is that we must all empower, and lift up each other. As a result of her WHY, she sought coaching certification and founded KATwellness Koaching LLC. Her approach to coaching is grounded in a focus on health & wellness, Dr. KAT asserts that there is no career wealth without foundational health. She is often called a "career strategist" and her methods for career advancement are well regarded. Dr. KAT empowers faculty women who desire to achieve tenure, get promoted, and be paid their worth without sacrificing their personal relationships, health, or wealth. Her big idea is that women in faculty positions are successful by virtue of securing those positions not just successful when they achieve tenure or get promoted. She asserts that pay equity for women must be established in academic circles.

Connect with Kimberly at https://about.me/Dr.KAT.

CHAPTER 10

On Your Power

Kimberly Robinson

"**G**et down from that tree, Kim, before you hurt yourself," my mother used to yell. "I have told you about climbing those trees! It's dangerous!" I responded, "Yes, Mom," and patiently waited for her to disappear so I was out of her eyesight, to climb back up to enjoy the fun of being an adventurer climbing the tree branches. I never fell out of any tree I climbed, because I was careful to use my eight-year-old brain to carefully analyze each limb, hoping it would hold my weight. I could not give up on getting to that thick limb, the one that was high up on the tree. God protected me!

> *For you shall go out in joy and be led forth in peace;*
> *the mountains and the hills before you shall break*
> *forth into singing, and all the trees of the field shall*
> *clap their hands.*
> ~Isaiah 55:12 ESV

As I climbed, I always hoped the limbs would not clap their hands. I needed stillness.

Throughout my childhood, I always enjoyed movements. Whether that was roller skating, climbing trees or playing kickball. Movement was what I loved. I felt as though I could never get enough of it.

I think it all came from my mother. She used to love to dance. I grew up listening to The O'Jays, Earth Wind & Fire, the Isley Brothers, and Peaches and Herb, to name a few. And she used to love moving around the house singing, dancing, and cooking. I used to love moving around the house, watching my mother smiling, singing, and dancing. I used to eagerly join her dance routine.

My Movement Changed.

I felt like the birth of my son was the beginning of my fight for the things that I truly desired in my life. I used to think, "How in the world am I going to really be able to focus on a job when I have a child? Who am I going to trust to take care of my newborn son?" When I spent my six weeks with him and had to go back to work, I cried the day that I had to leave my newborn. I didn't even drop my son off to be cared for until sometime in the afternoon. I finally dropped him off with my sister. She was kind enough to allow me to let him stay at her house, since she was available to look after him that day. I told the daycare center that I would bring him the next day.

I finally had to come to a moment where I had to trust God, that whoever took care of my child would not harm him and that was hard, because trusting people that I did not know was a very difficult thing for me. I had to trust God, so that I could go back to work and not lose my job.

When the next child came, life was a lot easier because I was a bit more accustomed to childcare. When it was time for baby #2 to be dropped off, I was glad. I was thinking in my mind, "Wow, I get a break." It was a much different experience. My only daughter came next. She was so much easier than the boys, very quiet, but she wanted to be with me all the time. That made it kind of challenging to get things done, at times. About three years later, I had a son. That' s a grand total of four children five and under! That was quite an experience. There were plenty of beautiful moments, despite the tough times.

God is our refuge and strength, an ever-present help in trouble. ~Psalm 46:1

I finally learned to ask for help. One thing that really helped me was having a few helpful friends that asked me if I needed help with anything. I said, "Yes," at times, but you know, there were a lot of times I did not ask anyone for assistance. That is what caused me to get so overloaded with things that I needed to do. About seven years later, I had more children and I was blessed to marry my husband, Larry.

I told him, "There's four here with me, you have two and that's a total of six. I'm good with that." But, I knew in his heart that he really wanted more children. He left the decision up to me. After some days of thought, I said, "Let's do this." We had a son. My husband was so elated!

Of course, most of us parents say, "I love my kids so very much." However, in the back of my mind, I was thinking, "How am I going to get a chance to do anything? How am I going to get a chance to focus on a career that I would like to work in? What would I really like to have for myself?" I felt clueless as to how I could truly take a real break.

My husband is so gracious though, he helps so much with all of the children. He gives me a lot of great advice on things to do to help things to run better. He reminded me that I should not be the only person in the house doing most of the chores. Time for the kids to get more involved.

What I really love about my husband is he really took a lot of the load off of me and explained to me how important it was to them that they learn the importance of doing things. That is one thing that really helped me. I constantly was trying to take the load off of them, but then after a while I was thinking why am I doing that? Maybe what my husband was saying was actually true, well I knew it was true, and such beautiful things begin to happen.

I have two sets of kids, plus a bonus set. That's how I describe it because of the age differences. I have one set from a previous marriage, another set from my current marriage and the bonus sons I received simply by being married to their father. That is eight altogether. Yes, eight is enough for me.

The first set of kids and I got to spend a lot of time together. It was just me and them for a few years; a time when I felt I had to do everything. Once I got remarried, my new husband reminded me that the kids were capable of doing more things than I had them doing. They became engaged in jobs around the house. I taught them how to cook some things as well. This helped me tremendously. The first set of kids helped me with my second set of kids.

How awesome that was! The second set of children developed a lot of the same habits and likes that the first set of children have. The first set loves to draw. They can draw well and are all artists. I truly believe that they are all great at telling stories and most of them love to write.

With the help of both my husband and my children, I now have an opportunity to start thinking about some things that I really have been wanting to do with my life. Once my children got in the habit of getting their work done around the house, I felt like I had some time to breathe.

I then decided this much: I love to work with groups of people. I would love to work with people in some way, where I can help them live better lives. What that actually meant, I wasn't so sure of at first. I used to watch a show called, *The Biggest Loser*. It was very emotional for me, watching everyone have so much weight on their body and then to get the opportunity to lose it. I was not sure what happened to everyone years later, but that was definitely a concern that I had in my mind for these people. I was thinking, "Wow. There's got to be a way that people can be helped after they lose weight to maintain their weight loss." And then my husband wanted to become a vegan after watching a documentary on Netflix called, *What the Health*, where he saw what was going on with the animals, how they were processed before they were taken to stores for us to buy and eat the food. He was horrified and he decided to become a vegan and he is pretty much still a vegan, other than eating eggs and fish occasionally.

Well, hooray for him. He gets to eat better, but what I was thinking about his decision was, what does this mean for the entire family, because my husband was thinking and saying, "You all need to consider going vegan." I am thinking about having the boys go vegan. Note: the first set of children are all grown and gone by now. And even though I can't say I am a person that feels as though they have to have meat, I was very concerned about the children, because I wanted to be sure that they got the nutrition that they needed. Then I started thinking, "I'm going to become a health coach." I have been looking at that for a couple of years, just thinking that that would be a nice thing to do, because it's such a great way to live. To really watch what I eat and know that that can help to prevent so many diseases. It has been on my mind for a few years. I said, "I'm going to do this."

I signed up for a holistic health coaching class with the Institute for Integrative Nutrition (IIN). I took the course, became a certified health coach, then I felt more informed. The boys and I, we practiced the vegan lifestyle for a while, even though we do have chicken twice a week, egg whites and fish occasionally, but other than that we were pretty much a vegan family. When I first started the journey, I saw how there were different ways that protein could be placed in the kids diets so that they were getting the protein they needed, but I still felt that it might be good for them to get a little bit of chicken occasionally. My husband and I talked about that. We talked about the soy and what soy could do for boys, but the thing about soy is that soy doesn't have to be bad. If you know how soy is processed, that is really what makes a difference in soy and there's so many things, so many factors concerning soy. That's why it wasn't always easy to tell whether I was getting good soy or not at the grocery store, but that's why I suggested to my husband that they eat a little bit of meat. That's what we do now. We all like to eat vegan meals. I'm so thankful that I discussed it with my husband and didn't just let things go. I really discussed the importance to him, of the protein and other things in their lives that I thought was good for them to have and he agreed, because he definitely researches, as well.

Even though I was a health coach, I felt like something else was missing in my career. I love working out. I love movement more than working out, I would say. I am so thankful for the time that I served in the United States Navy, because that was the place where I found out how much I actually enjoyed working out. My first week at my last Duty station, I had a sponsor that took me around. I did everything that she did. She said, "Hey Kim, do you want to go exercise? That's what I normally do." I was thinking, that sounds like that would be fun. So I told her, "Of course."

I went with her and she said, "Let's just stay in the back because this guy, he is a killer. We can stay back here and you can watch what everyone else is doing to help you stay up with everybody else and we can hang out in the back of the class in case we don't get all the moves."

The instructor was rigorous. It was so much fun and I was able to keep up.

At the end of the class, he greeted me and said, "Hey, you did a great job, especially considering that this was your first time." I replied, "Thank you." He then asked, "Have you ever thought about leading a class?" I replied, "No." He said,

"That's something you want to think about." I looked at him like he was crazy. Then he said to me, "You know, you should really think about it, because I'm going to be getting ready to leave here. I only have another month or so left here and we really need some more people to do this. We are short on time. If you're willing to do it, I will give you the music you need and I can help you set up a routine, just let me know." I smiled at him and said, " Ok," not thinking that I would do too much of anything at first. In my mind, I'm thinking, "What do I know about these people? Everybody's going to be looking at me. I've got to do something. What if I screw it up, then what do I do?" And then I remembered something that he said that motivated me a little bit. He said, "You can make a little bit of tax-free change on the side." I thought to myself, "That might be worth putting myself out there. Why don't I see what happens? What's the worst thing that could happen?"

I contacted him after a few days and told him that I would like to take him up on his offer, if he was still willing to help me out. He was elated. We got together and worked everything out. I had my first class and I cannot express the joy and the fun I had doing it.

Have you ever had the feeling, after doing something, that you would do it for free? That is exactly how I felt. I taught my first aerobics class with joy and vigor. I feel as though everyone enjoyed it as much as I did. My favorite day was the day that the commander of the entire Navy base decided to come and exercise with us. The gym was filled, I would say probably close to 60 to 70 people showed up to exercise. We had a ball! It was so fun watching the commanding officer try to stay in pace with the group! I thought he did a pretty decent job considering that was his first time out there. What we did back then was called aerobics, so we all were having fun aerobically!

I wanted to get back into the group exercise training for a few reasons. We get to work out together, do something good for our bodies and have fun! My remembrance of all that fun is one reason why I decided to finally become a personal trainer.

It took a few years before I made any efforts to pursue my career. My main concern was my time with kids and the things that I needed to do with them. I started homeschooling my youngest son a few years ago and I wasn't sure about my time.

What I've learned is I get to manage my time. I will definitely say that I'm no expert at that, but I feel as though I'm getting better each and every day that I decide to take action. I now try to start off with time for myself. I actually log the things that I do. I'm doing better at it. I make time for myself even if it's just 10 or 15 minutes to have a hot tea and take a few deep breaths. That has been making a difference for me.

And we are writing these things so that our joy may be complete. ~1 John 1:4 ESV

It delights my heart to speak of the hard things I have done, so that those who may be going through them right now, can be encouraged and inspired so that they can achieve the life they want as well.

I am so very thankful that I never gave up. I never gave up on my dreams, I didn't even know really what my dreams were. I didn't even take time, at first, to think about my dreams. I was thinking about what everybody else needed me to do and wanted me to do. Finally, I took a breath and thought about what I wanted to do. Once I did that, it still took me a while to make the change, but when I did I said, "I will never ever give up on doing those things that I know God wants me to do, because when I leave this life, I do not want to be a person that did not fulfill the things that I was called to fulfill." Who would want that?

And with energy to do things, you can use it to take action. Action is what makes things happen.

One final word. If you really want to never give up on your dreams, give your burdens, your anxiety, your fears and frustrations to God and trust that He will keep His word to you.

> *Trust in the LORD with all your heart, And lean*
> *not on your own understanding; In all your ways*
> *acknowledge Him, And He shall direct your paths.*
> ~Proverbs 3:5-6 NKJV

Kim Robinson

Kim Robinson is a Holistic Health Coach and Personal Trainer that specializes in helping clients change their mindset to tone their bodies, lose weight, gain energy, and increase mobility. Kim Robinson also loves to help clients develop simple breathing techniques and prepare delicious meals full of plant foods. Kim Robinson has a meal prep group where she shows ways to make delicious meals that are simple to prepare. When preparing meals, Kim Robinson loves to grab plant food from her aeroponic vertical garden. Kim Robinson fell in love with it and now she adds the Tower Garden to her offerings.

Along with the Tower Garden, Kim Robinson also offers concentrated fruit and vegetables to help the body get the nutrients that it needs.

Connect with Kim at www.mywellnessmatters.life.

CHAPTER 11

From Great Grief, Great Joy Can Come

Kinga Hipp

I would never have believed this when the accident happened, but here I am years later, and I can say that from great grief, extraordinary joy can happen—it is possible. I am a reluctant traveler on this journey, but it is my journey to take, and it is a path few take. I am learning to not give up on life, to continue persevering.

I will begin where my original journey ended and a whole new journey began, one I did not want to be part of. The first thought I can remember after the accident was, how am I going to do this? How can I survive this? I remember thinking, *I cannot live in this world without my son.* I wanted to die and be with him. The pain of losing my child was unbearable. It is hard to put it in words, but my whole body ached with physical pain. It is said that when you lose a parent, you lose your past, and when you lose a child, you lose your future. I lost my future that day. It was and still is the worst day of my life when my son left this world. It has been a terribly slow process, but I am learning to persevere and not give up on life.

Let me start with the arrival of my son into my life. He was born on an early spring day. I remember the day being warm and sunny, a perfect day because he was born. One of the best days of my life. My son was born at 10:48 p.m. Labour was painful, but the delivery was quick. As my son grew, he liked to wander, looking for the next adventure around the corner.

I did not worry about my son being as adventurous as he was because he was smart about things and careful. Even that fateful afternoon, I did not worry that he was going out for a ride on his ATV (quad). Before he went out for his ride, we had a conversation about this tragic bus accident that had just recently happened and how much money had been raised for the families involved in the accident. We went outside, and I got busy doing yard work. After a while I started to wonder why I could not hear his ATV. My husband jumped on another ATV and went to check out where he was. He came back shortly, but it felt like an eternity. He was distraught and said to me, "I think he is dead." He ran into the house and called 9-1-1.

At that moment, it was the end of the life I had once known and the start of a new one. I was now part of a club that no parent wants to be a member of. All I wanted to do was curl up in a ball and die, give up on life. There were some interesting moments that happened right after the accident. They can be described as *not a coincidence*, little miracles, mystical interludes, or *come on* moments. My favorite description of them is *you just can't make this stuff up* moments. The reason I like this one is that any time I experience one of these moments, I will say, "You just can't make this stuff up." The description of these types of moments has evolved over the years. If it were not for these little *you just can't make this stuff up* moments, those early days would have been unbearable. I would have given up on life.

One such *you just can't make this stuff up* moment was so memorable. My sister-in-law and niece had come to visit to try to comfort us. We were sitting in the living room near the fireplace when my niece said, "I hear a bird in the fireplace." I ran over to the fireplace, and sure enough, I could hear the frantic flapping of wings. I was like, "We have to rescue it." My husband, daughter, and sister-in-law came rushing over, and we were deciding what to do. My husband put some gloves on and bent down to look up into the chimney. We held a blanket over him and the fireplace opening, so the bird could not fly out and escape into the house. After a couple of tries, he yelled, "I got the bird." We moved out of his way as he made his way to an open door. He held the bird gently, but firmly in his two hands. He went outside, opened his hands, and the mourning dove flew away from his hands. It was an instant moment of pure joy, something I had not felt since my son's accident. I asked the people who had lived in the house for twenty years before us if they had ever had anything like this happen, and they said, "No, never." Since that day, it has not happened again. It was a joyful moment.

It is said that the sign of a mourning dove is hope, love, and freedom. This was a sign for our family. The mourning dove had left us with four feathers. There was one for my husband and I, one for his sister, one for his aunt and cousin, and one for my son. It was a beautiful moment, something you just cannot make up. It is still so vivid in my memory; I can see the graceful dove taking flight and me crying with joy. It was the first time in days I felt something other than intense grief and wanting to give up on life. It was still so early on, and I just did not think I could do it.

I remember thinking, *I cannot do this on my own. I need help.* We contacted the hospice association in our area, and they found us a grief counselor. It was the start of my healing. It was good talking with someone who was not a friend, a relative, or someone that knew my son. Also, she was a professional, and she knew what to say and not say. It was someone I needed in my life at that moment.

In one of my sessions, I was telling my counselor about attending my graduation ceremony. Although I was not partaking in the ceremony, I watched my fellow classmates cross the stage and receive their college diplomas. I was so proud of them all, and it put a smile on my face. My counselor asked me if I felt joy and happiness for my fellow students. I said with wonder, "Yes, I did," and she said to me, "See, you can experience joyful moments even with your great grief." It was an *aha* moment. It was a start; it was a baby step in my healing from grief. I was learning to not give up on life.

There was another session with my counselor that I remember well. I told the counselor I wondered why I did not know my son was in trouble that day. Up until then, I always had a sixth sense if one of my children was in trouble, but that afternoon, nothing—no worry, no apprehension. When the counselor asked me why I did not sense something was wrong, I had to think about it for a while and then responded to the counselor, "I think I wasn't supposed to know that he was in trouble." The universe had a plan for me, and I was not supposed to know at that point that something was wrong. This realization helped a little, it helped a little to not give up on life.

I was numb that first summer. I received a book from a friend called *Healing After Loss: Daily Meditations for Working through Grief* by Martha Whitmore Hickman. I have reread the daily meditation each day every year since the accident, which is five years. As I read each day, sometimes it seems like I am reading it for the first time. All the messages relate to grief, but some resonate more than others and at separate times. A particular day was March 3rd, and the quote for that date was:

> *As I begin to see beyond the pain, I sense how both sadness and joy are part of the tapestry of my life. ~*
> Martha Whitmore Hickman

This is the theme of my life since the accident. I have immense grief, but I am learning I can feel joy too, all intricately woven like the complex tapestry of my life.

The daily meditation book has helped with my grief and to not give up on my life. I started to watch a show that first summer called *Jane, the Virgin*. There was a scene with the main character and her grandmother talking about grief. The grandmother says,

> *Which is to say, you're in a long-term relationship*
> *with grief, but it has to evolve, it's okay to keep*
> *letting go.* ~ Grandmother, The CW's Jane
> the Virgin

Who would have thought I would hear something so profound from a lighthearted romantic comedy-drama series, but it is a quote that has resonated and stayed with me. It is so true about grief—it is a long-term relationship that I have with it, one I will always have, but one I can let go of a little bit at a time as time goes on. I am learning every day to live with grief and never give up on my life.

The first summer came and went. That first fall, I started a new job, which was a blessing in disguise. I began working in the school system as an education assistant, helping students in classrooms and supporting other students in separate ways at the school. It was a distraction from my grief, a kind of therapy. I remember driving to and from work crying about my son, but while I was at school, I was almost okay. I would never forget about my son, but at least when I was at school, he was in the back of my thoughts. I felt almost normal at school. I did not share my story with many at school as this was a new part of my life, a new journey, my secret life. People at school did not know who I was and what my story was, and I preferred it that way.

I still do not share my story with many people. This part of my story is so private and precious to me. I will share with someone if I am ready to and if, at that moment, it feels right to tell. I believe this has been one of my coping mechanisms. Working in the school has been incredibly good for me. I am needed at school, and it has given me a purpose to continue to live, to not give up on life. It has helped tremendously with my grief.

Another coping mechanism for me is knowing that I will be with my son again. It is not a belief; it is greater than that. I cannot really explain it; it is just something I know. This may be a survival technique, but whatever it is, it certainly helps to not give up on life. It may be faith, although I am not religious. Spiritual, yes. Religious, no. As time passes, after five years, I continue to be sure that I will be reunited with my son.

Along the way, I have learned much about grief and how it can affect so many aspects of one's life. One, of course, is to not give up on life and persevere to live. As my husband and I were trying to deal with our grief, we attended a conference about near-death studies. There, we met a lady who, too, had lost her son, many years earlier, and she gave us two pieces of advice. One was to remember that the second year was much more difficult than the first. The other piece of advice was, as a couple, we had to work extremely hard at our relationship because many couples split up after the death of a child. We took this to heart and have worked on our relationship, realizing that each of us is on our own journey and we deal with grief differently.

It has been a lengthy journey, and I imagine it will continue to feel like a long time, until I am reunited with my son again. I try to take it one day at a time. I try to live in the present moment as it is only the present moment that I am in control of. I try not to reflect on the past too much because the past is the past, it has happened, and I cannot do anything about it. I work very hard at not worrying about the future because it, too, is something I cannot control.

Something else I learned was that I could not control the outcome of what happened to my son. The what ifs that surrounded the accident were abundant. I was trying to figure out how I could have changed the events of that day. We should not have let him go for a ride on his ATV; maybe I should have just hugged him all day and not let him go outside. The what ifs are so detrimental to anyone's healing process. They serve no purpose to dwell on them; they only make one feel worse. There is no point to them, because they do not change the outcome of what happened. I have learned to not put any energy into the what ifs.

What I did put some energy into was friends. Some people who were acquaintances surprised us and became good friends. They understood us and would say and do what we needed. They just got us, and it was so appreciated. Then there were other friends who distanced themselves because they could not handle it. No one wants to acknowledge the potential of losing a child. No one wants to think about that or have it as a reminder. It was as if we had some fatal contagious disease people did not want to catch. It was like, *if I see them, I might catch what they have.* From this, though, I have learned what a devoted friend is and what is important in a friendship. Years have passed, and I have some good friends.

It has been five years, and I still dread the anniversary date of the accident and the days leading up to this date. I recall a dear friend telling me, "The time leading up to significant dates is always the worst, anticipation of what I don't really know." The words ring so true for me. Since the accident, I have anticipated this day with such apprehension, and once it comes and goes, I realize it is just a day, not a significant day. As time goes by, I wonder if this day will become less significant to me.

Time is an interesting notion. Does it really exist? Is time a fabricated concept made up by us?

Time does not exist—we invented it.
~ Albert Einstein

For myself, during this journey, there are times it feels like the accident happened just yesterday, and at other times, it seems like it was an eternity ago.

Early on, I mentioned the tragic bus accident that happened just before my son's accident. Recently, I read a news story about this tragedy. It was a memorial to the accident that happened five years ago. It was a devastating crash that took the lives of sixteen people, mostly teenage boys. They were a hockey team traveling to a game when an eighteen-wheeler truck hit their bus. I remember at the time of this bus crash how sad I was for all those families. Little did I know that two weeks later, I would experience my own personal tragedy. I could not believe when I read the story that it said it had been five years, which means my son has been gone for five years as well. It really surprised me because it does not feel like five years, but then other times, it seems like life has been so very long without him.

There are still times I feel guilty for having happy thoughts and experiencing joyful moments. I think to myself, "I should not feel good, I should feel sad and dreadful." This has been another aspect of grief that is so hard to get away from. The guilty feeling usually creeps up when I am feeling happy and experiencing joy, and I think to myself, I should be miserable, not happy. It is a constant battle in my mind between feeling content and feeling sad. I am still learning that I do not need to feel guilty. This journey I am on is a continuing learning experience, and I must remind myself that it is okay to be happy, to love life, and not give up on it.

I have learned much in the past five years, since my son's accident. I have been put on this path, my current journey, for a reason. With my knowledge and experience, I am becoming a grief counselor. I have found that helping others with their grief helps me with mine. It is a win-win situation. I want to help others with their grief, and hopefully, with my help, they can find some comfort, they can be at peace, and they can find joy. I believe this is my next chapter, the right step for me. I am still learning. This has been a long, tough road, and although I have learned so much and have been given many wonderful gifts, if I could have my son back, I would give it all up in a heartbeat. I know I cannot do that, though. I know I will continue to have grief, but I also know now that I will experience joy. I will continue to not give up on life. I will persevere.

Kinga Hipp

Kinga Hipp was inspired by her son to write about her journey. Although her son is beyond the veil, he is very much part of her life. Kinga lives in Kelowna, British Columbia with her husband and daughter. She spends lots of time in the great outdoors with her two lovable dogs.

Connect with Kinga at khipp@telus.net.

CHAPTER 12

Navigating Life's Rollercoaster

Secrets to Building a Life that Feeds Forward
Kohila Sivas

As I lay in the hospital bed, my mind was filled with questions.

How had I ended up here?

The answer to that question was a long and painful one. My journey towards that moment had been difficult and full of challenges that no child should have to face.

At the age of 13, I had experienced more than most people should in a lifetime. The weight of it all was crushing, and I found myself constantly thinking about giving up and asking the question, "What's the point?"

It's hard to imagine what could make a child feel this way, but for me, it was a combination of living amongst a civil war, losing my grandparents, moving to a new country with cultural isolation, racism, language barriers, an alcoholic father, and the abuse of someone I trusted.

All this built up for so long until one day, it consumed me. I felt so lost and alone. I remember sitting alone in the park, my heart heavy with the despair that had been building inside me for far too long. I felt the weight of the world on my shoulders.

I had lost hope. I had a bottle of pills to relieve the pain that consumed me. My mind was filled with a mix of emotions - sadness, anger, frustration, and hopelessness.

I had many conversations with myself that day. I thought of all the people I would miss, the ones who had shown me kindness and love throughout my life. I couldn't bear the thought of leaving them behind, but at the same time, I felt like a burden to them.

I also thought about all the things I would never become, the dreams and aspirations that now seemed so far out of reach. The sense of loss was overwhelming. In that moment, I felt like no one would care when I was gone. There was something inside me that refused to live.

So, when I found myself in a hospital bed, I was struck with a sense of disbelief. I learned later that against all odds, I had been resuscitated.

It was a strange feeling, to be suspended between life and death, unsure of which way to go. I stared up at the white ceiling above, and I was filled with emotions. Part of me was relieved that I had survived, that I had been given a second chance at life. Another part of me was angry, angry that I had been stopped, that I couldn't even control my own destiny.

I felt trapped, a prisoner in my own body. I felt like I was drowning, suffocating under the weight of my own thoughts and feelings. In the midst of this darkness, there was a glimmer of hope. That I was still alive and breathing meant that there was a chance for me to turn things around. It was a chance for me to start over, to begin anew.

Something inside of me refused to give up. For the first time in my life, I recognized and understood the power of the mind. I realized I had been talking to my brain through those conversations with myself. Little did I know this experience would become the foundation of my coaching methodology, the Meta-Learning DeStress Method.

This dark moment marked the beginning of a journey that taught me the true power of perseverance and resilience in the face of adversity. I had to fight through pain and suffering, but I knew that I had to keep going, no matter what.

So, I made a promise to myself - a promise to keep going, to NEVER give up. Even if the road ahead would be difficult and filled with challenges, I knew that I had to keep moving forward.

As the days and weeks passed, I began to see that there was more to life than the pain and darkness that had consumed me.

Looking back now, I realize that my experience, in that hospital be, was a turning point in my life. It was a wake-up call, a reminder that life is precious and that every moment counts. I am grateful for the second chance that I was given, and for the opportunity to make a difference.

When I finally re-entered the world, my attitude and energy were different. I struggled at school, but then I discovered mathematics, and when I discovered how I could use it as therapy. I channeled my energy and focus into it.

*It's not that I'm so smart, it's just that I stay
longer with my problems.*
~Albert Einstein

These words gave me hope. I didn't need to be smart. All I needed to do was commit to spending the time to figure it out.

With this newly found knowledge and with a focus on talking to my brain, I was able to excel in math through hard work and determination. I started hacking and cracking the code of math. Math was my passion, and I pursued it with all my heart. It was through this pursuit that I found a sense of purpose and direction in my life.

After completing my education, I became a teacher so I could share my methods with other students.

However, I soon found that the traditional education system didn't suit me. I felt frustrated and limited in my ability to make a difference in the lives of my students. I knew I had more to offer, and I began to explore how to create my own environment.

I started my own tutoring business, but soon I found that it wasn't enough. I was driven to create something that would truly make a difference. So, I began to dive deeper into the message I received on the day I lay on the hospital bed after my suicide attempt.

This is when I started to formulate and develop my coaching methodology, drawing on my experience and expertise in mathematics, as well as my own struggles and challenges. I refined it over time, until it became something truly unique and effective, the Meta-Learning DeStress Method.

My journey didn't end there.

Today, I train and certify teachers under my methodology, sharing my expertise and experience with others who want to make a difference in the lives of their students. Through my work, I have been able to touch the lives of countless people, helping them to find their own purpose and direction. Collectively, we are on a mission to serve 1.5 million or more students by 2035.

When I entered the entrepreneur world, about eleven years ago, marketing was a challenge that held me back and kept me stuck. I had hired many so-called experts who promised everything, but delivered little. I learned many hard lessons from my failures. Instead of giving up, I applied myself to learn marketing, just as I had learned math.

When I found success, I launched my own marketing agency, using the same approach that had brought me success in other areas of my life. Now I have added AI to power my marketing strategies.

Through my company, Holistic AI Marketing Agency, I am positioned to help passionate coaches, authors, or anyone with an amazing superpower build their own thriving business. My mission is to help others achieve their goals and realize their potential.

Looking back on my journey, I have learned a few key lessons along the way:

First, NEVER give up. No matter how difficult the road may seem, there is always a way forward. Even when things seem hopeless, there is always a glimmer of light that can guide you towards a better future.

Second, focus on your strengths and your superpowers. Identify the areas where you excel and find ways to use those strengths to create a better life for yourself and those around you. You don't have to be naturally gifted; you just have to stay longer with your problems to find the solutions.

Third, be open to change. If something isn't working, don't be afraid to try something new. Sometimes, it's the unexpected twists and turns in life that lead us to our greatest successes.

Fourth, surround yourself with supportive people. No one can achieve success on their own. We all need the support and encouragement of others to help us through the tough times and celebrate the good times.

Finally, believe in yourself. You have the power to overcome any obstacle and achieve any goal you set your mind to. All it takes is a little bit of perseverance and a lot of hard work.

Here's my gift to you, my acronym N.E.V.E.R. G.I.V.E. U.P.

N - Never let fear hold you back. Fear is a natural emotion, but it shouldn't stop you from pursuing your dreams. Acknowledge your fear, but don't let it paralyze you. Use it as fuel to push yourself forward.

E - Embrace failure. Failure is a natural part of the journey towards success. Don't be afraid to fail - embrace it as an opportunity to learn and grow. Every failure is a step towards success.

V - Visualize your success. Imagine yourself achieving your goals and living the life you've always dreamed of. Create the NEW YOU that you want to be and shift your habits and mind stories to achieve it.

E - Empower yourself. Take control of your life and your destiny. You have the power to create the life you want, so don't be afraid to take risks and make bold choices. Believe in yourself and your ability to succeed.

R - Resilience is key. Life is full of ups and downs, but it's important to keep going even when things get tough. Shift your mind stories and develop a mindset of resilience and perseverance, and NEVER give up on your dreams.

G - Gratitude is important. Take time to appreciate the good things in your life, no matter how small. Thank you is the most powerful weapon to your success.

I - Invest in yourself. Take the time and effort to develop your skills and knowledge. Invest in your personal and professional growth, and don't be afraid to seek out help and support when you need it.

V - Value your journey. Your journey towards success is just as important as the destination. Celebrate your accomplishments along the way and take the time to reflect on your experiences and what you've learned and achieved. Every moment in your life is purposely placed for you to learn and grow.

E - Energy and effort makes a difference. Success requires hard work and dedication, but it needs to be fueled by positive energy. Creating positive energy comes from learning to talk to your brain. Only you can coach your brain.

U - Use setbacks as opportunities. Don't let setbacks derail your progress. Instead, use them as opportunities to learn and grow. Keep pushing forward, even when things don't go according to plan.

P - Persistence pays off. Success rarely happens overnight. Stay persistent and keep working towards what you want, even when progress is slow. With persistence and learning to coach your brain, anything is possible.

If you NEVER GIVE UP and focus on the opportunities that challenges present, you can achieve great things in life. Whether it's finding your passion, starting a business, or making a difference in the lives of others, we all can create a life that feeds forward and helps others.

Along the way, remember to NEVER give up on your life or on your dreams. Embrace the gift of N.E.V.E.R. G.I.V.E. U.P. and keep moving forward.

I hope my story and my acronym will guide you on your journey to success. Everything is solvable.

As I reflect on my journey, I am filled with gratitude for the experiences and people who have helped me along the way. From the hardships that once consumed me, to the moments of triumph and joy, every experience has taught me something valuable about life, myself, and others.

I am grateful for the power of my mind, which has allowed me to overcome challenges and pursue my dreams. Through my work as a teacher, a coach, and an entrepreneur, I have been able to make a positive impact on the lives of others, sharing my knowledge, experience, and passion to help them reach their full potential.

I am grateful for the support of my family and friends, who have been with me through the highs and lows, providing love, encouragement, and inspiration. They have believed in me even when I didn't believe in myself, and I am blessed to have them in my life.

I am also grateful for the power of technology, which has enabled me to connect with people around the world and share my message on a global scale. Through my Holistic AI Marketing Agency, I can help others achieve their dreams and make a difference in the world.

As I look to the future, I am excited about the possibilities that lie ahead. I am committed to continuing to learn, grow, and evolve, and to sharing my knowledge and experience with others.

I am passionate about helping others find their purpose and direction in life, and I am dedicated to making a positive impact on the world.

So, let me end this chapter with this quote:

Success is not final, failure is not fatal: It is the
courage to continue that counts.
~ Winston Churchill

You have the power within you to overcome any obstacle and achieve greatness. It may not be easy, but it's worth it.

Remember that success is not just about achieving your goals, it's about the journey you take to get there. Embrace the challenges, learn from your mistakes, and keep moving forward.

Life is precious, and every moment counts. So, live your life to the fullest and NEVER give up on your dreams.

Keep pushing forward, and always remember the power of N.E.V.E.R. G.I.V.E. U.P. With this mindset, you can transform your life and achieve anything you set your mind to.

Now, it's your turn. What challenges are you facing in your life, and how can you apply the lessons from this chapter to overcome them?

Take a moment to reflect and set your intentions for the future.

Remember, everything is solvable, and with the power of N.E.V.E.R. G.I.V.E. U.P., you can achieve your wildest dreams.

You have the power within you to create a life that feeds forward and makes a positive impact on the world. N.E.V.E.R. G.I.V.E. U.P

Kohila Sivas

Kohila Sivas, the founder of Learning Success Coaches, is a dedicated professional who helps teachers and educators achieve success in their careers. Kohila's coaching methodology is designed to empower educators to develop the skills, knowledge, and confidence they need to enhance student learning outcomes and run their own successful coaching practice.

As an online holistic Learning Success Coach, she specializes in providing coaching services to students of all ages and their parents. Using her proven and tested Meta-Learning DeStress Method, Kohila tailors her coaching process and methodology to meet the unique needs of each student and family.

Kohila's expertise doesn't end with education. She is also the driving force behind Digital Genius AI Marketing - a cutting-edge business that offers comprehensive digital marketing solutions to businesses of all sizes.

Kohila's ultimate mission is to serve 1.5 million or more students by 2035 and to help businesses of all sizes launch and make an impact and increase income. Whether you're an educator looking to enhance your career, a student striving for success, or a business looking to revolutionize your marketing efforts, Kohila has the expertise, experience, and passion to help you achieve your goals.

Connect with Koliha at
https://www.learningsuccessacademy.com/.

CHAPTER 13

From Surviving to Thriving

Latara Dragoo

So, there I was ... stranded smack-dab in the middle of Baja California ... literally. I had very little, other than the shirt on my back, and was trying to walk back home. A few moments earlier, I was in the passenger seat of a truck. My much older fiancé was taking turns strangling me and punching me in the face, while driving erratically through the bowels of a foreign country. He was not happy with the answers I was giving him.

The trip had started out well, like a dream. We spent the first week camping and fishing on the beach and watching dolphins jump in the distance. Some local boys, the sons of a fisherman, walked into the water, equipped with garden hoses, grabbing up sea cucumbers and giant scallops off the floor of the Gulf of Mexico, and tossed us a couple of scallops the size of my fist, just because we were there.

From that magical experience, we drove to the tip of Baja, and I had requested a brief stop so I could get a great photo of El Arco ... the iconic rock arch going down over the dramatic waves where the Pacific Ocean meets the gulf. The water actually drops down several feet, and the two bodies of water can have contrasting colors and current directions ... it's an amazing sight, for sure!

When he found a spot on the side of the road to pull over, the only view I had was the bottom of a ditch and some pseudo-industrial looking building obscuring the view. Unfortunately, I mentioned this, which insulted him greatly. Have you ever been on a long road trip with someone, and you start grating on each other's nerves over little things? Somehow, from the time we drove from the southern tip of Baja to about halfway back up, towards the border, our conversation had retrogressed to a highly volatile banter in which we were emotionally reacting to each other's insensitive quips.

At this point, he was convinced that I had lied when I told him that, several months earlier, his father had hit on me. He was irate, feeling I said this in order to manipulate him and break his family apart. I told him, multiple times, that I was telling him the truth the whole time. He disapproved of this answer and decided to resort to physical violence to unearth the truth interrogation-style. He asked if I lied about his dad. I said, "no." POP, right in the face, was his response. This scenario repeated itself several times ... He went off on a rant with his hand wrapped firmly around my neck, and then returned to the question again. This time, I thought that if I recanted my earlier confession, he would relent from his course of action. He asked if I lied about his dad. This time, I said, "YES." POP, the same response as before ... At this point, I am unsure what to do. I was in survival mode and was willing to do or say whatever it took to preserve my life.

Since whatever answer I gave was clearly unacceptable, I decided that my best option was to jump from the vehicle, which I did. He slowed down temporarily, to what felt like around 35 miles per hour, and I launched out the door, somersaulting as I hit the ground, and immediately leapt up and started running in the opposite direction. He pulled a U-turn and backtracked towards me. The universe had blessed me with an outcropping of bamboo nearby, which I crawled into to hide. He jumped out of the truck and started walking in my direction, still screaming for me to answer the question about his dad. At this point, all I could do was scream back, "I don't know!"

I repeated it over and over and crunched myself even further back into the thicket of stalks. He gave up on trying to crawl in after me, and finally decided to leave, while yelling out indignantly, "Good luck getting the hell out of Mexico!"

Fast forward to 2020 ...

First off: Obviously, I survived!

Secondly, I am now a branding and marketing strategist and consultant. I was laid off from my job as Assistant Publisher of Dream Homes Magazine when the COVID shutdown occurred at the end of March 2020. After having worked for the company for over 18 years, just like that, my career, my symbol of security just went poof. At this point, while most of the world had shut down, in the most literal term, I immediately decided to pivot. I started my own corporation in April of 2020, and brought in a couple of coaches, as well. While I know every aspect of publishing, I had little experience in sales, and I knew that if I was to become a successful business-owner, I needed to not only be competent, but also able to effectively sell my services.

Unfortunately, it does take a slight bit more than just passion, a message, and desire to help others. You need to find a vehicle, (or several) to send your message out to the world and find your people. For example, my sister has a master's degree in fine art. She was so impassioned about pursuing her artistic endeavors, that she went to school for 10 years to do it. I was shocked and amazed over the fact that in all of her extensive years of training, that a class on how to market and promote her own work was never on the curriculum! It doesn't really matter what your passions are, or how talented or knowledgeable you are, you still need to promote yourself, sell yourself. Otherwise, you end up, like the majority of people, with a college degree naively entering the workforce with blind hope. Then they find themselves in a job that had nothing to do with their degree - their burning passion, and instead settling for a position of convenience. As evil as they say money is, most people would agree that you need money in today's society to just get by day to day. In my opinion, it's much better to do something you actually like doing for a living, to make that money.

That is why I wanted to help others, whether they are starting on their entrepreneurial journey, or they are a small business owner who is struggling to keep their doors open and their dreams alive during the shut-down, and beyond. Many people simply hunkered down, waiting, and hoping that we would return to normal. The sad part is, I don't believe we can ever go back to how things were before. We are entering into a new paradigm. We are also entering into a redistribution of wealth - a new economic shift. Those that are able to quickly adapt, and even embrace this *new normal* are going to be the ones who end up not just surviving, but thriving, once the COVID dust is finally settled.

In the vein of being a light at the end of the tunnel for those seeking a new way of life, I am offering up several tools for people who, like me, have decided to take advantage of our capitalist society by becoming their own boss. We in America, in particular, have a certain degree of freedom to pursue our own business ventures. Self-made individuals that recognize the opportunity in adversity are the ones that will rise to the top while the rest huddle, paralyzed in fear and denial, unable to take action when it is needed most.

You may think I am speaking pure nonsense. If you take a look at points in history, during recessions and turmoil, those were the times when the great historical icons created themselves by rising up out of the grime, adversity, and ashes like legendary phoenixes.

Turbulent events are those instances where the wheat gets separated from the chaff, the cream of the crop rises to the top, or what-have-you. These self-defining moments make or break you. The more prepared and equipped you are to take immediate action, the better off you will be, long term.

The ultimate measure of a man is not where he stands
in moments of comfort and convenience, but where
he stands at times of challenge and controversy. ~
Martin Luther King Jr.

Now back to the Baja story...

I wandered along the road for a time when a car pulled up slowly behind me. I started to try and run, but as the adrenaline rush from the previous experience was wearing off, my legs felt like lead - like in one of those odd dreams where the more you try to flee, the more stuck in slow motion you tend to be. I gave in. May as well concede to my fate, as I had little hope of escaping this time. The man in the black car pulled up and started talking to me in Spanish. There was no chance of communication, but he opened the glovebox and a stack of church programs spilled out. He then pantomimed a collar around his neck and pointed to the back of one of the programs, and I was somehow able to decipher that he was a priest of the church. So, I got into the car. He tried in vain to converse with me, but then took me to a house. While I stayed in the car, he summoned the resident. She came out and introduced herself as Esther Collins. She spoke broken English and relayed to me that she was a deacon of the church, as well as the head of two orphanages - one nearby, and one closer to the border, near Ensenada. I spent the night at her home, and the next day, I rode in a crowded car with her to Ensenada. From there, she bought me a bus ticket to the border. I walked across the border in Tijuana, then boarded the trolley in San Ysidro. I was now depleted of funds, and the trolley ticket taker was making his rounds. He asked for my ticket. I did not have one, and he asked me to get off at the next stop. I think the giant black eye I sported caused him to take pity on me and not press any charges against me for my insubordination.

Luckily for me, my dad's house was just a hop, skip and jump away, in San Diego County. I arrived on his doorstep and waited for nightfall. When he came home from work, I jumped out of the bushes yelling "Surprise!"

Even though I had run away from home so defiantly and insultingly, at the age of 16, he welcomed me back into his life, years later, without skipping a beat. It was almost as if that entire chapter of life, of rebellion, and subsequent remorse, hadn't even happened. It was like I was coming back home from a day trip. My dad simply hugged me and said, "Come on in. Let's have some supper!" Because of my family's unconditional support, I was gradually able to pull myself up off of the floor and make something of my life.

Looking back at my harrowing escape in Baja, I made some life-changing realizations; God is watching over me. Of all the people that could have picked me up, and with kidnappings and foul play running rampant, I was picked up by a priest, and aided back to the US by a church deacon! I realized I was part of a bigger plan.

From this experience, a seed was planted. I did not want to be beholden to a man! Leading up to this sudden break in our relationship, my ex would often hold over my head that I was living in his home rent free. The fact is I was only there because he brainwashed me against my family, and I had left the safety of my home and loving family to be with him. And he reminded me I was eating his food, despite the fact that weeks would go by when I was eating little more than fritters that I would fry up using cornstarch and flax seeds in a pan of vegetable oil. At the time, I had no way to repay him, as he would not allow me the autonomy of getting a job of my own. As a result, I was basically held prisoner, feeling like I was indebted to him for his astonishing generosity and hospitality!

Surviving hard times, we become stronger. They say that events like that *build character*, and I suppose it is true. I decided from that point on to seek out a career, so that I was never dependent upon a man for room and board again. And while sometimes, I find myself jealous of those fortunate women who were able to get married to their high-school sweethearts and become stay-at-home-moms, I don't think my staunch independence would have ever allowed me to thrive in that lifestyle.

I have worked my way up the corporate ladder in the real estate industry, then worked for a small business in the luxury publishing niche. I eventually found myself in Assistant Publisher status after almost two decades of dedication. I then found myself breaking away, once again, and tackling a clean start as my own boss - now even more independent than ever, but not alone. While filled with trepidation about the new journey, I also have an unwavering optimism that I will succeed, no matter what reality throws at me, because I know God is watching over me, and I am part of a bigger plan!

Latara Dragoo

Latara Dragoo is a Graphic Designer and Marketing Strategist and consultant who specializes in helping entrepreneurs, small business owners and coaches to brand like a billion-dollar company. With 18 years in the luxury publishing industry, 20 years of experience in marketing and graphic design, and 10 years in online marketing, Latara is well-equipped to meet her clients' needs. She dedicates her time to helping clients create a strong online presence and attract their ideal clients.

Her ultimate goal is to help busy, non-technical small business owners and coaches thrive in the new normal by providing outside-the-box, win/win solutions for their #1 problem in their business. If you need help getting your vision out into the world, Latara is here to bring it to life, and connect you to your target market in the digital world.

Connect with Latara at https://linktr.ee/latara.dragoo.

CHAPTER 14

Never Give Up!

Laurie Bodisch

Introduction:

Life is full of twists and turns, and my journey to becoming a badass business owner was anything but straightforward. Parts of my story are glorious while others are so painful that it's taken me until now to share my *Never Give Up!* journey with you. Over the years, I've found that when we share our stories, it gives others a chance to tap into their own resilience and unique gifts. Your past doesn't define you. It's just a part of who you are.

The Early Years:

I was born in a small New Jersey town, where my dad worked three jobs, while my mom stayed home to take care of my brother and I until we started kindergarten. We spent weekends with family, and occasionally made day trips to Sandy Hook beach or drove into New York City to see a Yankees game. Playing school and being a pretend math teacher was one of my favorite pastimes as a child. From a very young age, I knew I wanted to be a schoolteacher. I loved to learn. My parents even made sure that when we moved to Pennsylvania, I had a huge blackboard in the basement, so I could keep figuring out my math homework, as it got more complex!

While I was young I developed a passion for baton twirling that proved to serve me well over the years. I earned college scholarship money as Pennsylvania's Junior Miss, won the Intermediate Miss Majorette of America title, and became a majorette captain in the Penn State Blue Band. What I didn't realize at the time was that the more I achieved, the more I felt the need to be perfect.

When I was a junior in high school, my dream of becoming a teacher was crushed. My guidance counselor insisted there were too many teachers in the system and encouraged me to pursue a different field. So, in my freshman year at Penn State, I enrolled as a computer science major.

Finding My Way to Finance:

Despite my best efforts, computer science never really clicked for me. I needed to find a field of study where I could interact with people, not just a machine. So, I switched to the business college, changed my major, and graduated with a Bachelor of Science Degree in Finance.

From a very young age, my mom always told me how important it was to have a career of my own. She wanted me to be financially independent, so I would never be forced to keep a job I didn't like, stay in an unhealthy relationship, or rely on anyone else for money. I would be free to make my own choices and be the driver of my destiny. This was the best advice ever!

Struggling in a Male-Dominated Industry:

My first job in the financial brokerage industry was as a support specialist. I vividly remember sitting behind a counter where my official title was wire operator, but I was really a glorified order-entry clerk. On the other side of the counter, there was a room full of men, who were on the phone telling their clients what stocks to buy and sell. This was in the mid-1980s, and the online trading platforms we have today didn't exist, so anyone who wanted to buy or sell a security had to go through a stockbroker. My question from day one was, "Why are all of the stockbrokers men?" I watched and learned all that I could.

A few years later, my personal situation took me to a town about 100 miles from where I lived. I secured a job as a sales assistant at a well-known brokerage firm, but I was still doing administrative work for one of the big money producers. This company sponsored me to study for the Series 7 exam, the behemoth in terms of being legally licensed to buy and sell securities. I passed the exam on the first try and my title was upgraded to a registered sales assistant, meaning I could give clients investment advice, but I was being paid a salary to do mostly administrative work.

Life took another turn and I landed a new position as a full-time stockbroker at a small, regional firm, where I was the only female registered representative at the firm (and in the town).

It didn't take long for me to find out that being a woman in this new capacity was going to be hard. In the early 1990s, cold-calling was the way to find new clients when you were a newbie stockbroker and a transplant from another city. Most men I talked to didn't take me seriously as a financial professional, even though I had all of the licenses and, most times, more education than my male colleagues. I was told that I was either too young to know what I was doing, or that I should be at home making babies and building a family. I found myself constantly overlooked and disrespected simply because of my gender. The icing on the cake was the day my boss offered to buy me new bed sheets, so we could roll around in them together. Yep, a grown man with kids of his own.

Over the next decade, my hard work paid off. I secured a branch manager position, which meant I was not only responsible for my own clients, but also supervised all of the operations involved to ensure the brokerage office was compliant with regulatory rules and best practices. I created marketing campaigns, dealt with personnel issues, and stayed current with continuing education requirements. I took exams for so many licenses and certifications that it makes my head spin thinking about it.

At the age of 32, I was honored to receive the Central PA Forty Under Forty Award and was surprised to find out that a wonderful couple, who were clients, took it upon themselves to nominate me for the award. They always told me how thankful they were for my investment advice and friendship, but I never truly realized how much of an impact it had until that moment. The following year, I was humbled to be named one of the Best 50 Women in Business in the state of Pennsylvania. Life was good.

In 1998, I was blessed with the greatest gift of all. I gave birth to a precious and beautiful baby girl. I was living a wonderful life, and believed I was doing all the right things necessary for a successful career and family.

Amidst the pressure to keep the momentum going with both family and business, as well as the now constant need to be perfect, there was a dark demon taking more and more from me. I was using alcohol as a coping mechanism for stress and it was beginning to spiral out of control. I was literally killing myself, both on the inside and outside, but couldn't see it. I was in denial.

Taking Control of My Life:

It was at this point that my entire family intervened, and in 2003 I spent 30 days in an alcohol addiction rehab facility. I was literally forced to stop and take inventory of my life. I was filled with shame and regret and lost relationships with people I considered to be true friends. I swore I'd never fall into that dark place again, because more than anything, my daughter deserved to have a sober mother.

Lots of changes happened in my personal life, and I eventually reunited with and married my high school sweetheart after 25 years. It was one of those fairytale love stories that you see in a movie or read in a book.

Unfortunately, I fooled myself into thinking that I could have a drink again and be just fine, but it didn't work that way for me. I relapsed and this time, I was going to lose everything.

That was my absolute rock bottom. And that was the last time I've ever had a drink.

People ask me what changed this time around. I usually explain it by using a very basic concept that is also a foundation of every investment portfolio I manage … risk and reward. Generally speaking, the greater the risk of an investment you make, the greater the potential reward you reap, but also the greater the potential loss. When I apply that to my life, the greatest risk I could ever take would be to have a drink, but there would never be a positive reward. It would be a complete loss of everything I value most in life. So, there is absolutely no chance that I'll ever take that risk again. Take a moment to think about the risks and rewards that impact your life. What risks do you take in everyday life? Are you getting rewarded appropriately for those risks?

I've also managed to find internal peace by letting go of the need to be perfect. A mantra I use is "done is better than perfect." And I don't let the bad actions or crappy mindset of others assume space in my brain. I used to do that a lot. Each day, I find at least one thing I'm grateful for and write it down in a journal. Some days, I fill an entire page with a thought, but most days it's a sentence or two.

Getting Back to Work:
Once I was ready to integrate back into the working world, I decided that I was going to pursue my childhood dream of

teaching and I became a certified substitute teacher at the secondary level. With the best of intentions going into this phase of my life, I found myself doing what many substitutes are told to do ... show the students a movie or make the class a study hall, which felt like babysitting 101 for high school students. I knew this would not be a permanent gig.

Eventually, I found my way back to finance with a renewed energy and focus as a business development officer for a local bank. Given my past investment experience, I was asked to join the investment department as a vice president in the wealth management group.

Never having lost my yearn to learn, I stepped-up my game. I spent three years earning a CTFA™ (Certified Trust and Fiduciary Advisor) advanced certificate and another three years studying for the CFIRS® (Certified Fiduciary and Investment Risk Specialist) designation. I helped high net-worth clients create complex investment and estate planning strategies that aligned with their unique goals. These included luxurious trips abroad, funding their child's or grandchild's education, purchasing vacation homes, buying expensive cars, enjoying their retirement years, and ensuring that their assets would pass to their heirs and favorite charities in the most tax-efficient way possible.

Most of my clients were kind, hard-working people with successful careers. I found that more often than not, men had some knowledge of how the markets worked (or at least pretended to) and were generally in charge of the household finances. But, when it came my female clientele, a majority of them lacked financial acumen and confidence about money.

Over the years, many professional female colleagues from the banking and other service industries that came into my office, closed the door, and asked for help deciphering their 401(k) statement. They knew they were supposed to be contributing to this plan, but were embarrassed that they didn't know how it worked and if they were *doing it right*. I continued to wonder why we, as intelligent, professional, ambitious women, don't talk about money and wealth in our everyday conversations? Men brag about how great their investments are doing and how much money they're making, so why don't we do the same thing?

After doing a lot of research and case studies on the topic, the answer was often the result of something we were told or had experienced when we were young, and our brain made it the rule (the norm).

Here are a few phrases that may sound familiar from your childhood:

- Pat, it's not polite to talk about or ask people how much money they make.
- Amy, you know that all people who have money are bad and are going to hell.
- Brenda, your dad takes care of the money stuff.

So of course, it's not going to be natural to have conversations around saving, investing, and building wealth.

It was around this time that a co-worker introduced me to an online academy that helped people learn about entrepreneurship and starting a business. It sounded intriguing. Friends and clients always told me that I should teach investing, because I had a way of making money make sense. I began to ask myself, "Could I actually do this?" I imagined the ways that I could use my experience and expertise to have a greater and more direct impact in teaching women how to build wealth. But, then that all-familiar doomsday gremlin would appear on my shoulder and yell "Stop! Who do you think you are? You will never make it work. You're not good enough to be a business owner. Don't you remember all the mistakes you've made in the past?" Then, I just let the idea go and figured I was too old to start a new chapter in my career.

Recognizing The Perfect Storm:

In 2017, my dad passed. Fortunately, my parents' legal and financial documents were in order and they had a secured document with all their passwords prior to his death. My mom didn't have the burden of making any hasty decisions. But, she was forced to deal with the emotional pain that comes along with widowhood. My dad loved photography and took tens of thousands of pictures through the years. He was the keeper of the family photos and stored most of them on his Apple computer. Why do I share this with you? Because when he died, we realized that the password to his Apple computer was not on the password document. The photos were lost because Apple won't help you retrieve a password. It's a devastating lesson that no one else should ever have to face.

Now my daughter was in college, diligently preparing to start her own career and become an amazing asset in corporate America. A place that can eat you up and spit you out in a moment's notice, especially when you're a woman. What else could I be doing to help prepare her?

Then I met a woman, who I'll call Mary for privacy considerations. Mary and her husband (I'll call him Jim) both had successful careers. Mary was familiar with her 401(k) plan through her employer and had her own fun-money account, but that was about it. Jim, who managed the personal finances, was unexpectedly hospitalized and died a month later.

Mary couldn't stop crying the day we met and kept saying how embarrassed she was for not knowing more about their financial situation. She didn't know which bank had the safe deposit box, how many bank accounts were actually open, or what investment accounts they had. She knew their wills and trust documents were up-to-date, but didn't know if they were in the safe deposit box or stashed away in a drawer. The list went on. This woman was forced to learn about finances quickly, and during one of the most emotional times of her life. She didn't know where to start, but eventually, we sorted everything out. Unfortunately, she wasn't as well-off as she thought. She needed to learn about investing. And unlike my mom, she didn't have a "Laurie" to help have these things in place before Jim died.

The three events I share above, are the true driving forces that convinced me there was a gap in the marketplace for women who wanted to be better and do better with their money. I realized how much of an impact I could make and how incredibly rewarding it would be to help motivated women build wealth and protect their loved ones. I was scared, but in a good way. There's always a risk and fear of failure, but honestly, it didn't compare to the immense satisfaction and joy I'd get from nurturing women to be financial powerhouses (remember my earlier conversation about risk and reward?) So, at the age of fifty-six, I officially retired from my corporate position and Her Wealth Coach™ was born!

Starting Her Wealth Coach™:

Starting a new entity takes a lot of time, financial commitments, legal hurdles, and faith to make it all work. By being intentional about what I wanted my money to do for my family and myself, I've been able to make my dream a reality.

I develop my own courses and programs, because I know what it takes for a woman to build wealth in the twenty-first century. I'm a confident leader, progressive financial planner, and badass investment fiduciary. My clients are motivated high-achievers and are ready to elevate their money game. They have big dreams they want to slay and make a reality. Most make great money, but aren't quite sure what to do with that money or how to make savvy financial decisions with confidence.

As the founder of Her Wealth Coach™ I'm so darn proud to be positioned as a premiere women's educational empowerment company. I'm on a mission to provide tailored customer focused solutions that help women gain the self-awareness and financial confidence necessary to take control of their own narrative. I get to show up as my authentic self every day and help other amazing women build and protect their wealth. I've come full circle in my quest to be a teacher and I will never let my past define my future.

Reach out if you're ready to level up your wealth game and Never Give Up on your dreams!

Laurie Bodisch

Laurie Bodisch is not only an accomplished business owner and financial expert, but a true trailblazer. She's the Founder and CEO of Her Wealth Coach™, an educational empowerment company that provides personalized financial consulting as well as group mentorship and coaching programs tailored for professional women. Her mission is to ensure that these women feel completely in sync and confident when it comes to building and safeguarding their wealth. With over three decades of expertise in Investment Management, Financial Planning, Trust Creation and Social Security Strategies, she's already transformed the lives of countless women, helping them take charge of their financial futures.

Laurie's passion for empowering women extends beyond Her Wealth Coach™. She currently serves as the president of the Board of Directors at the Gate House, a non-profit addiction recovery care organization, and is a member of several professional organizations including the York Polka Dot Powerhouse and the Penn Square American Businesswomen's Association. Laurie holds a Bachelor of Science in Finance from Pennsylvania State University as well as FINRA licenses, advanced degrees from The Institute of Certified Bankers (CTFA™), Cannon Financial (CFIRS®), and the National Social Security Association, LLC (NSSA™). With her diverse skill set and experience, Laurie continues to make a significant impact on the lives of women, empowering them to be financially secure, wealthy, and unstoppable.

Connect with Laurie at www.herwealthcoach.com.

CHAPTER 15

I've Given Up on Giving Up

Lynnette LaRoche

Here I am, back in San Francisco after pursuing a job opportunity at a pre-IPO biotech. It didn't work out. Although the founder and I were a great fit, and the board thought so, as well, he was getting less than stellar advice from a friend.

I'm on my third boss at the job. Another, "Oh, why did I do this to myself?" The company toots itself as being all new, but it is just a spinoff from the parent company. Otherwise, how can a company be new when there are people who have worked there 10, 15, 25, 35 years?

I have three huge programs, one of which has delivered favorable data, which means we will be filing for drug approval. I pour myself into my teams, my employees. Seeking out development opportunities, helping them grow their leadership and careers. I love 95 percent of them! I have made good headway into the remaining five percent.

I am known for innovative ideas and exceptional leadership skills. I've built strong performers at my previous two companies and am replicating that here. I've built this strong performance culture through relationships and communication. I've never used a video cam!

Yep, I love my team. Just not the job, the company. I don't see a future here for me, at least not a future where I can grow and climb the ladder. I have been constantly feeling the twinges that there has to be something more for me. Something that I create. Something that I own.

It was a beautiful night at my house in Twin Peaks, San Francisco, in September 2019. The moon was in the sky and I could see the lights on in the buildings downtown, reflecting glittering light onto the bay. It all sets the scene for a relaxing and peaceful night, but I was feeling antsy. I had had a successful run in the biopharmaceutical industry, being known for building high performing teams and expert planning. I had just bought my fourth home and I had traveled significantly to many parts of the world. I had material things. From the outside looking in, people might have thought I had a great life. Yet, I was feeling like I was just existing.

I screamed out to my friend the moon, "What am I here for? What am I supposed to be doing with my life? Give me a sign!"

Whilst looking for some binaural beat sleep music, there is a commercial with Tony Robbins and Dean Graziosi for *Knowledge Brokers Blueprint.* I watched it all. I bought in. That was the beginning of this journey into entrepreneurship!

At that point in my life, I was a workout addict! It was the only thing that I ever really had to talk about. Naturally, when I started this new journey, I zeroed in on helping mid-life women who were beginning to feel the aches and pains of aging and weight gain. I worked with them to reclaim their lives and I didn't stop there.

It's time for an interlude.

So, I have moved back to San Francisco, my expenses have increased 33 percent and I haven't found the right job for me. Crap! As if I hadn't already depleted my savings buying the house well over asking, I was spending more money, because I needed to get away. So back to Santorini I went for my birthday. Greece, that is.

I love Greece. Santorini is my soulmate island. I feel very grounded, even whilst traveling alone. It speaks to me. I let go. I trust. I am a woman alone, in and around the island.

I experienced beautiful nights, watched the sun set into the Caldera. Stars winked at me in the sky. On lovely mornings, I sat having breakfast whilst watching the cattlemen herd horses and goats through the steep, slippery, stone stairwells, and narrow pathways. I took in beautiful boat rides, where I saw incredible, white-washed houses atop the cliffs. I felt so much peace and freedom.

It was short-lived. It was time to go back to work.

Over the next two months, I was pulled in multiple ways at the job, not only on my projects, but working on potential acquisitions, as well. I was double, triple-booked for meetings. Whilst all of this is going on, I am refining my niche for my own business. What do I want? Who am I in this space?

I almost lost the deposit on the San Francisco house. Although I was able to sell my home in San Diego, I was not yet divorced. The bank would not allow me to close on the house in San Francisco without being officially, unmarried. They needed to be assured that my ex would not show up later and make a claim to the property. Understandable. At first, I panicked, but I pulled myself together to focus and figure out what I needed to do to resolve this issue and protect myself financially.

I mention this, because I was receiving legal papers with a last name I didn't want. I was defining who I was as a single woman. One who was no longer looking outside herself for what she needed, and that included, my name.

My maiden name wasn't mine. It wasn't my Dad's. It wasn't my grandfather's, either. It was assigned to him. So, what name did I want to identify with?

I'd always had a love affair with France. As a child, I always thought I would live there. I had reserved the opportunity to go to Paris until I could go with the love of my life. Instead, my first visit to Paris was a few months after separating from my husband. I enjoyed a month in Paris, but I didn't love it. It became a month of routine, checking off the list of things to see and do.

I go back to Paris during Christmas on a name-finding visit! It's cold, but this time I am enjoying Paris. I released from a few lifetimes ago, a vow of marriage I had made to a fiancé who had died at sea whilst in the military. I visited several significant cultural locations and museums for surname inspiration. There were names that I held love for and resonated with, but I felt people would be challenged pronouncing and spelling them, being that on a daily basis I have to correct people on the spelling of my name. I did not come away with my new surname, but I did have a renewed view of Paris.

So, back in San Francisco I'd found that, although I loved this city, I knew it wasn't always going to be home.

Work was becoming even more intensive and intrusive. My programs had been elevated to enterprise critical, so even more was expected of me and hence the more I expected of myself and my team. I task my team with the ability to withstand the asks. In my other world, I am still navigating entrepreneurship.

I have always been passionate about helping people. I didn't realize it at the time, but I had a gift for intuitively knowing the needs of others, developing, listening, and offering guidance.

I had been in a mastermind group and one of the coaches there asked why I was avoiding building a business with the expertise for which I was known. My gifts were developing employees into high performers and building high performing teams and next-gen leaders? I didn't see it as anything special. Surely all people managers had this skillset, right?

From then, my focus evolved to helping high performing women, whose health or personal lives were suffering, to achieve work/life harmony. Bringing them back to wellness. Help women break out of the small mindset and create the impact for HERstory. I shifted into digital marketing, becoming a messenger boat-building maven.

Being that my intent was to build a business that would replace my corporate job income, I shifted to helping women break free from the golden handcuffs of corporate business to become their own bosses.

At first, things seemed to be going well. I was so excited and poured all of my energy into it whilst working corporate hours. I spent countless hours building my website, creating content, and reaching out to potential clients.

As time went on, something was just off. I wasn't seeing the growth that I had expected, and I wasn't making the kind of impact that I had envisioned. Despite all of my best efforts, I wasn't getting the results I anticipated. So, I began to speak with other successful entrepreneurs, sought out mentors, and hired coaches to help me grow my business. I listened to advice such as you must surround yourself with successful people who were in the same industry or who had relevant experience. Except that no matter who I spoke with or how much money I invested, I couldn't seem to make traction.

At first, I was super excited to be working with such experienced and influential professionals. I had believed their guidance and expertise were the seasonings I needed to achieve my goals.

I was told to focus on the pain of potential clients, to position myself in a way that would make people want to collaborate with me. I was encouraged to talk more about the problems I could solve and less about my own journey. Write content focused on their storyline, not my own. Another advisor had me writing content that was similar to output from a google search. Wooden!

Oooh, I thought that niche won't work or it will be hard to find clients, so I should focus on another niche. Still another would throw statistics at me saying most people fit into this space. I'm not most people, but I felt like I had to listen to their expertise and heed experience, even though deep down, I knew that it wasn't right for me. Darn *need-to-fit-in* and I *want-them-to-accept-me* genes.

I was told I needed to speak like this and look like what the market demanded to attract clients ... to change ... me. Being a good student, I tried to implement their strategies. I went along, doing THE things, but eventually I would hit a wall. I would then beat myself up mentally for not being able to pull it off. For not being able to keep it going. For not being successful.

I doubted myself and my abilities. I felt worthless. I felt lost and frustrated. I was used to being successful in corporations, but as an entrepreneur, I was not cutting it. I felt like I could not raise the bar for myself. I was tired of feeling like I was wasting my time and money on something that wasn't going to work.

As the money dried up, so did the support. I didn't see, at the time, that I wasn't making traction or seeing sustained success, because I was sacrificing and compromising who I was.

So, there I was again, screaming up to my Moon, my namesake, "Why am I doing this? Why can't I get it right? What do I not see?"

Despite the advice of others, I chose to move back into my authenticity. I am talking more about my journey and what led me to become a coach and consultant, sharing my struggles and wins.

I had to walk away from people who were not aligned with who I am, even if it meant losing money. I had to trust that the right people would come into my life when the time was right.

This has not been an easy road. I invested more than $150,000 over 18 months in consultants and coaches that treated me like a plug and play, not seeing who I was or understanding my vision.

I felt like I was constantly starting over, resetting my baseline, and chasing a dream that was always just out of reach.

I've made massive learning opportunities, not failures.

I used my own funds instead of pursuing small business loans or grants and a $200K renovation had depleted my nine-month living expenses savings, leaving me with nothing to live off of. However, using my own funds may not have been a bad thing had I not spent massive amounts of money BEFORE my business was ready, before it was generating income.

I learned that I couldn't take successful people's advice as gospel, because what worked for one person might not work for another. They don't always know what's best for you and your business, and you should take only that which serves you.

I learned that my *need-to-fit-in* gene was alive and well, which caused me to allow other's opinions on how I could be most impactful overrule my instincts and vision. Saying *yes* even though my gut was telling me *no*.

I learned that proximity is not always good for you if proximity is not relevant to where you are in your journey. I equated general proximity, or need to get in the room to be exposed to the people, to driving on the freeway. If you get off at the wrong exit, you are confused, frustrated, and need to backtrack to get back on track. I learned that if proximity will cost me time, money, and energy, but no ROI, then I won't get off at that exit. I will keep driving.

Being an expert planner and premier portfolio director in corporate only translated so far in the entrepreneur space. I learned that I can't treat entrepreneurship like a corporate business, where money can be spent to reduce timelines and fast-track success.

Perhaps most importantly, I learned to trust myself. I learned to trust my own voice, my own inner knowing, and my own journey. I learned that I didn't need someone else to save me or tell me what to do. I have everything I need, within myself, to create the life and the business I want. Only I can create my success.

I had to let go of the focus on misses and refocus on what was going well. I had to focus on my unique perspective, voice, and vision. It's a good thing that I'm not like everyone else. I had to stop trying to fit into a mold and create my own.

I don't blame the experts I worked with, as they were only doing business. I am fully accountable for everything that happened to me on this journey.

I temporarily threw in the towel a few times. I'm not giving up. I am too determined to succeed. Not for others, but for myself. I'm determined not to live a good enough life, but an exquisite life. So, I persevere, take risks, and trust my own voice.

Reset five, seven, eleven ... or so. So, I finally did a thing. I asked for something. Yes, I also learned that I am not always supposed to give, that it was okay to receive. So, I have a mentor. Someone who sees me. No money attached!

I have paused at this moment on prior niche pursuits. I know my IT will unfold and it will allow me to create a beautiful tapestry of travel, wellness, women's empowerment, mindset remapping, and fashion. A business that will be a portal of fun and liberation for me and my clients. Uniquely and exquisitely me. Although I will address the pain potential clients are experiencing, my business will not focus exclusively on this aspect. It will paint the compelling future which will be expressed through my stories and through stories shared by clients.

As an entrepreneur, it can be easy to get lost in the noise and the advice of others, especially when one seems to contradict another. It's essential to remind yourself why you started in the first place and have the courage and resilience to press through, even in the face of challenges.

I remind myself of my past successes, I left biotech with two drug approvals, and the obstacles I had overcome in the corporate world. Entrepreneurship has setbacks the same as corporate, and although you may not have the massive resources available to you, as in corporate, the principles required to turn setbacks around hold true. I know that success is not just about making money, but about creating something that is exquisite, meaningful, fulfilling, and impactful.

Something beautiful to me.

This brings me back to my chosen surname. LaRoche means *the rock*. Very fitting. I had been *the rock* in my family growing up, defending my siblings. I had been *the rock* with friends. I had been *the rock* to my employees. I had been *the rock* to people I didn't know. But I had never been *the rock* for myself.

Now, it is time. I must be my own rock.

My vision is too important. I can see it, but I have not yet translated it.

I'm not giving up!

Lynnette LaRoche

After leading a very successful career in the biotechnology/biopharma industry, Lynnette LaRoche left her mark with two drug approvals during the height of the pandemic and a legacy of building and leading high-performing teams.

Lynnette is the founder of niche businesses whose mission is to enable clients to become a better version of themselves and recreate beautiful lives after a major transition. With a focus on guiding women as they embark on their first entrepreneurial journey, she is the architect helping their iconic vision come to life through her ß *iconic* venture.

Leveraging over 25 years in leadership, Lynnette also provides consulting to pre-IPO and small biotechs/biopharmas to create organizational transformation through the three pillars of: Leadership ~ Empowerment ~ Growth through her SCIgenuity venture. She develops leaderships' behaviours and skillsets required to lead in today's fast-paced, ever-changing environment, which are key to improved employee engagement and peak performance.

She is a speaker – she spoke at the London House of Parliament on World AIDS Day 2022 – and an international best-selling author. Lynnette is also the recipient of an Honorary Doctorate degree for Humanitarianism for Women's Empowerment from Global International Alliance, and holds multiple international awards.

Connect with Lynnette at https://3voluxion.com.

CHAPTER 16

Finding Your Purpose
By Accident

Melissa Kimmerling

nitially, when I discussed my story idea for this book, *Jumping Hills,* she wasn't familiar with the term. I replied, "You know, where you drive on dirt country roads - the kind that go up and down and up and down, and you try to get some air going over a hill? For a little thrill? You know, because there is nothing else to do?"

She didn't know. I went on to explain to her that long ago, I had grown up in a little farm town of about 1,600 people in rural Nebraska. The kind without a stop light. Where your neighbor was the music teacher and your uncle ran the local bar and your dad's service shop sponsored the yearly high-school-band-fundraiser calendars. It's where kids run around unsupervised and no one locks there door. It is where teenagers get into trouble.

I wasn't the kind to get into much trouble. My mother had died when I was 11 and my brother was seven. Since my dad is an over-the-road truck driver, this meant that I took on caregiving responsibilities pretty early in life. We had family around, as well as, what seemed to be a revolving door of dad's latest girlfriend. Looking back, I really think he thought that he was doing what was best in trying to find someone to care for us consistently when he was away.

At the time of my accident, my dad was married to my former stepmother. Like any grieving daughter, I kept myself closed off from her. I was not interested in having a relationship with her or her daughter, and I was furious anytime she moved a picture on the wall or re-arranged the living room. To keep myself out of that home, I kept busy. I worked at the grocery store, babysitting, and washed dishes at the bar. I was in drama, swing choir, and Academic Decathlon, and church group, and band, and pretty much any other thing that kept me busy. That is the perk of a small town- no competition. If you want to do it, you're on the team. When I wasn't working or busy with school activities, I drove around. We all drove around. Before cell phones and social media. We all *took mains* in hopes of seeing a friend, then promptly pulled over to the nearest empty parking lot to sit on the hoods of our cars and chat. And hopefully, be seen by someone way cooler than we were.

On July 18, 2000, a friend came by to pick me up to drive around. Like I said, totally normal at that time, and in that place. We picked up another friend, and then tried to pick up another. He was mowing his lawn and couldn't come. He was the lucky one.

We didn't go far outside of town. Just past the golf course that at the time, they were just building. I actually hated jumping hills, but like any teenager I felt victim to peer pressure and tolerated it anyway. The truck was dark brown and old. A 1960-something, maybe. I remember the way down the road. All was normal; a little air, a little laugh, and then we turned around. It was the last hump on the way back to town. I can still feel rising up out of my seat, then slamming back down, then the sick sensation of realizing we were rolling.

The next thing I remember, I am in an ambulance and asking them to stop cutting my clothes off. I was so embarrassed, but I hurt so much. I remember the small-town hospital in the next biggest town, with someone holding my arm out of the machine while they scanned to see the damage. I remember the next hospital, the trauma center in the city in which I now live. The same hospital where my mom died, just five years earlier. Waking up and finding something taped to my nose. "What was it?" I thought. Never mind, go back to sleep.

I endured eighteen broken bones that day. You read that right - eighteen. Five vertebrae, nine ribs, two arm bones, a clavicle, and a hip. They fixed my arm first, with an external fixator. If you've never seen one, they can be disturbing. The pins that hold your bones in place stick out of your skin and attach to rods that run the length of your broken bone. If that wasn't enough, they decided to surgically fix my spine by inserting two rods, four pins, and enough wire to hold the new instrumentation in place. I sit here on this date with all of that instrumentation still present. And because I was a teenager, all of those procedures were done without requiring my consent.

It's easy to look back now, and feel as if that is just a story that happened to someone else. That this person is a character in a book I read. I can vaguely see the hospital room if I close my eyes, and I see the scars clearly every day. I know in my core that this happened to me, but it also feels like a long-ago story I tell about someone I knew. You see, at that moment, I was faced with a decision; to let this event ruin my life, or to keep moving forward. Now don't get me wrong; I wanted to give up nearly daily, when I was still in the hospital. The physical and emotional pain were excruciating. I missed my mother terribly. There is something about your mother that even the most well-meaning auntie can't replace. Her absence re-broke my heart.

Things started to change when the rehabilitation team started their sessions with me. The occupational and physical therapists on that unit knew exactly what to do to promote the healing and return function to the trauma survivors on that unit. "I just got comfortable. Come back later," I would beg. "This is important, Melissa. You need to start working on getting better. The time is now." They pushed me just the right amount to get me up, moving, doing things for myself, and out of the hospital. I hated 99% of it, but before I knew it, I was home.

I had a second encounter with occupational therapy after the removal of the pins from my wrist. "They should have just cut my arm off," I said to the outpatient therapist after seeing how little function I retained. Good thing they didn't, as that therapist worked miracles. I fully admit that I wanted to give up on my therapy sessions so many times, but I persevered. Before I knew it, my hand was fully functional and pain free.

Little by little, I got another piece of me back. The more I could do for myself, the better I felt both physically and emotionally. Eventually that intense pain subsided, and I became used to a chronic ache that I retain to this date. This all happened at a pivotal time in my life, in between my junior and senior years of high school. This greatly impacted my decisions related to college, and I went on to pursue a career in occupational therapy. I now use my experience to influence how I motivate my clients and now, my students, to keep moving forward.

I went from that sad girl, in all that pain, to a strong female leader in my field. I lead two graduate-level occupational therapy programs, maintain clinical practice, and represent my field in policy and academic initiatives at a national level. I have a happy family and happy home. None of these accomplishments were without another opportunity to quit and choices to keep going.

It can be assumed that successful people somehow are free from challenges; that the world somehow is kinder to them. "How did she get so lucky?" Thoughts run through our heads when we see that tall, confident female lead a room like she had been there forever. Not knowing that that leader is unsure about her message, feeling self-conscious in her new suit, and stressed that she is missing her son's soccer game to attend this professional event. That feelings of, "Am I doing the right thing?" Soar through her mind constantly. That the last time she spoke, she got some negative feedback that she is still trying to process. But, she is back up there anyways, because she knows that if her story makes a difference to just one person that that will be enough. That she and her husband haven't had a date night in over three years. That she wonders if her teenage son is happy, and if her preschooler will start listening to his teacher anytime soon. This leader is the current version of me; one who is ever-evolving, needs support, and doesn't always have clarity on what comes next. The only thing I am really truly clear on is that I just need to keep moving forward, through the highs and lows of a life well-lived.

I often say to my clients, after they have experienced an accident, illness, or injury that "Life may not look the same after this, but that doesn't mean it can't be good. We just need to work hard, together, to help you meet your goals." We all are faced with decisions in our lives that force us to re-evaluate what is truly meaningful. The challenges we all face are part of the lived experience of being human. They open our eyes and hearts to the experiences of others, and we become more insightful and compassionate as we build our resilience. We see more clearly what is truly meaningful to us, and re-prioritize our lives to reflect our core values. We revise and refocus and recommit. We change the course, or try a different path, but keep moving forward. We evolve, learn, and grow. We face each challenge with a little more confidence and a little more belief in ourselves. We cry, scream, hug, and wish things may be different, sure. That is part of being human. But, we come out the other side and keep moving forward. We never give up. I hope that whatever challenge you find yourself facing now, you can find your way through it. Someday, the experience might just be a story you tell about a character in a long-ago story.

Dr. Melissa Kimmerling

Dr. Melissa Kimmerling is a graduate of College of Saint Mary, obtaining her BS in 2006, her Master in Occupational Therapy in 2007, and her Doctorate in Education in 2014. She currently serves as the Founding Program Director and Associate Professor for the Occupational Therapy Programs at Nebraska Methodist College. She also serves as the Vice President of Policy and Advocacy for the Nebraska Occupational Therapy Association. In this role, she supports the legislative endeavors of the state professional association, working closely with the lobbyist and chairing the policy committee.

Dr. Kimmerling also serves as the Nebraska Ambassador to the National Board for Certification in Occupational Therapy, which is the organization that administers the occupational therapy licensure examination. In addition, she serves on the Roster of Accreditation Evaluators for the Accreditation Council for Occupational Therapy Education where she reviews accreditation compliance of occupational therapy programs.

Dr. Kimmerling lives in Papillion with her husband, two sons, one dog, and two cats.

Connect with Dr. Melissa Kimmerling at https://bit.ly/kimmerlinglinkedin.

CHAPTER 17

Taking Back My Destiny

Najia Said

wanted to scream, "You're such a f-ing liar! How dare you treat me like I am stupid!"

There I was, sitting in front of the screen, on a zoom call, with my boss. She had set up a last-minute meeting with me, right before I was to have my team meeting to roll out some new efficiency processes and systems. I had been working on it for about three weeks. My meeting was supposed to start at 9 a.m. and I was pulled into her impromptu meeting at 8:15 a.m.

She started with, "You are not going to like this meeting."

I felt the blood drain from my face and panic start to rise. "NO, this cannot be happening!" I thought to myself, "I just started this job three months ago!"

Many emotions and panic crept in as I listened to what ended up being utter BS. "Sometimes skill sets just don't translate," she said to me. AS IF!

However, even though I was extremely upset, I knew I had to keep some composure. You could cut the tension with a knife and my body language was screaming discontent. My face was too. I sat back, crossed my arms over my chest, cocked my head to the side and pursed my lips as I listened to the lies she was spewing about my skill sets.

This was not the first time I was about to be laid off. It had become a new normal for the last two jobs I had had in the last three years. It was foreign to me the last 20 plus years in my previous industry but, now it seemed, a new pattern was forming. "Interesting," I thought.

Was she kidding me? This must be a sick joke. It has to be, because if she thinks I believe this load of crap, she must be out of her freaking mind. This lady was creating make believe issues about me to make herself not feel guilty. She was about to lay off a single mother with two kids. I had just signed a one-year lease on a new place, I had no more savings due to COVID, and it was less than 90 days since starting a new career path in this position. She had decided it was time for me to go. Three months.

She had never even taken the time to get to know me. Never had lunch with me. Never asked how I was doing. Nothing. Red flags for sure. That's all it took for her to decide I wasn't good for her team. She saw me as a threat. She was intimidated by what she saw in me. I was a powerful, outspoken, articulate, organized professional woman whose past experience was working in the construction industry. As a project manager, I had been running multi-million-dollar projects in a male dominated field and I had the resume to prove it. I was not an affirmative action hire. I was great at what I did. Period.

I almost had whiplash with how fast this all happened. I couldn't believe this was happening to me. What did I do to deserve this? I'm a good human. I treat others with love, kindness, and respect. Was this my payment?

By this time, a few minutes had gone by and I had had enough of her spiel. I was about to boil over, yet still felt very powerless. It was a zoom call, so I decided to take control and after a few words to her about her not taking any responsibility for any of her own actions, I said to her, "This call is over." I hung up on her. That felt good for about two seconds, then reality set in again.

I sat for a minute, and I could feel my brain swirling. I could feel the fear of the unknown future set in … then I felt RAGE. Deep rage that I was here again, having to figure out how to land on my feet. It wasn't fair having other people dictating how my life played out. That is what I thought at the time.

My kids were at school. They were finally back to in-person schooling after the COVID lockdown, so I was by myself, in my house, alone with all my thoughts. What am I going to do now? My mind was going a mile a minute. I was in survival mode AGAIN.

I took a pause and sat not knowing where to begin. I contacted only the necessary people: my ex-husband, my siblings, and my girls from my traveling group, who are my biggest cheerleaders. I knew they were all going to ask me, "How are things going with your new job?" Insert ironic chuckle here. The new job in a softer industry, which is more nurturing, more inclusive, and more understanding … what a joke! I explained humbly and vulnerably to everyone, "Please, don't ask me any questions about what I am going to do, because I do not have a plan at this point, and I need to think and re-evaluate my life." I was scared, I won't lie about that.

This was supposed to be my interim job as I reskilled myself on how to be an entrepreneur and build my way out of the oppressive corporate structure.

Fight or flight, that's what you do when you are scared. It wasn't like I hadn't been here before, but this time it was different. I felt the old pattern of panic and anxiety wanting me to start spiraling into a frantic abyss of scarcity, lack, insecurity, and a sense of doom. I had been there before. It was a horrible feeling, and I didn't want to repeat that part of my life. It was dark, gloomy, and lonely. It didn't allow me to sleep and the anxiety was unbearable.

Let me give you a quick snapshot of the unexpected and significant life changes that occurred between 2015 to present day 2021. (Clearing my throat) Toxic misogynist work environment in construction, short sale on our forever home, interstate move to try to save a marriage, emotional neglect, sexism, divorce, money scam, job layoffs, COVID, father diagnosed with dementia, death of my father, ADHD and Autism spectrum diagnosis for my kids, school bullying, school suspensions, racism, gaslighting ... that's off the top of my head. This was, without a doubt, the most impactful pivotal point in my life.

I realized I had to evaluate my life thus far, why was I here, what did I need to take control of what did I need to release control of? I also had to learn how to never again play into the hands of people, entities, and societal norms that do not serve me or my family. I needed to stop giving my power to others, and expecting them to create for me the life I desired, and then getting upset when they didn't get it right.

Ouch! That kind of smarted a little ... okay ... it smarted a lot. I first had to stop feeling like a stupid smart person with a deer in the headlights look, frozen and not able to choose a direction. I was not a young deer. I have skill sets. I have the ability to make good decisions. Decisions that would lead me and my boys to the best quality of life.

I decided that for the next steps, I needed to feel the fear and do it anyway. I had to make decisions, even if they didn't turn out as expected, I needed to be prepared to make another decision and keep taking action.

The theme of this book is Never Give Up. That is what I am doing. Giving up is not an option when you have two amazing kids, whom you want to raise to be even more amazing adults. Giving up is not an option for me. Initially, giving up, for me, meant the easy way out. Meaning, at first you throw your hands up, surrender, and say, "never mind, I can't go any further, I relinquish it all to someone else." However, when there is no one else and you love your children too much and you love life too much to continue to allow others to take control, you find the wear with all to take the smallest baby steps of steps to get you moving again.

Growth and learning do not happen in isolation. People may try to have you believe they are a self-made whatever … fill in the blank. Last I checked, you were born into this world by a woman and raised by, hopefully, at least a small village of family members, schoolteachers, mentors, good friends, professors, etcetera. If that is considered self-made, then everyone is self-made. Congratulations. I believe we as humans, were not created to be by ourselves, but to be connected and joined together to build fabulous things. That is our superpower.

So, there I was, June of 2021. I had just made a conscientious decision to try my best, to not hide behind shame and pride, but to seek guidance, resources, and anything positive from all sorts of avenues. I could then break through my limiting beliefs and hurt feelings. I was already an amazing, fully functioning, and capable human. After many years of micro aggressions and many overt aggressions, one can start to believe in the doubt and not their true abilities. When that happens, it will negatively affect the trajectory of your life.

I was determined to break free of those shackles and figure out who I was, all over again. I was not a fresh college graduate, naïve to the world experiences. I was now a college-educated woman with over twenty years in the construction industry, divorced with two children with special needs. I had a burning desire to scrap everything I was led to believe about creating a great life and explore a different blueprint for my new life of abundance. The challenge was, how.

Although it can be said that there are many things out of our control, such as how people think of us, which labels they put on us, bias, racism, sexism and all the other isms. The one thing that we can be in control of is deciding how we will choose to live the rest of our lives.

Once we decide how we want to be treated, how to take up the space we deserve, and start to work on our limiting beliefs, we can truly live the life we dream about.

I often find that the life we dream about is not something we keep on the forefront of our minds. Many, me included, were taught that a successful life is to go to university, get a degree, find a career, work 40 years, get married, have two point five kids, one dog, white picket fence, and you will live happily ever after.

At least that is how it was within my community circle growing up. Reflecting back on my life, I felt like I wasn't encouraged to really explore my true self. I do not remember anyone telling me not to, yet somehow, I fell right in line with the normal path of life movement. I finally realized, I could no longer shove myself into the round hole with my square peg. It didn't fit me anymore. Technically, it never did. It was always uncomfortable.

I was made for more!

No one really encourages you to be fearless, to spread your wings to fly, and explore before you settle down. I never liked that term. It always felt limiting. I would say, "I don't want to settle, I want to LIVE!" Live fully, live out loud, and enjoy the world with my kids. That was the dream anyway.

It was during that time in early June 2021, that I made it a mission of mine to find all the ways to shore myself up physically, financially, spiritually, mentally, and any other way I needed. I decided right then and there that I am too smart and too determined to have anyone or anything decide my life, but me.

The biggest challenge I faced was within myself, and whether or not I would allow outside forces to pull me away from unlearning a lifestyle. I no longer could fathom being in a role where I was forced to continue to feel that the only option out there was another job with a better boss.

At this point, I went onto social media and asked my friends for any and all podcasts that were recommended to improve one's mental health. I also downloaded books, and found different social media influencers to follow. My objective and lesson learned was to not allow my brain and thoughts to start taking me down a path of gloom, doom, and anxiety.

Anytime I started to focus on my lack versus my abundance, I reached out and engaged one of my many resources. Additionally, as things got tough, I used my therapist, a colleague that morphed into a mentorship, sorority sisters, social media community, local and distant friends, and family to help keep me propped up when I felt like falling or when I got scared and couldn't see the light at the end of the tunnel.

I kept going by remembering that I am a wonderful human being who is merely, in a moment of time, in the middle of a huge life transition. In reality, there was no way I could give up, because if I did that would mean all the powers that be would have won, versus me winning the life of my dreams.

I would often find myself, after many moments of what seemed endless negativity, going back and reading or watching other single moms' stories of triumph. In the end, we all win when we do not give up. We have to take the timeline away from success, no matter who may think there is one, including and especially yourself.

Changing the trajectory of my life has not been easy, but nothing worth fixing is ever really that easy. Especially, when you've invested so much time going in one direction. I equate it to turning the Titanic, but I will tell you this, even though I didn't completely miss the iceberg, this ship will not be going down. It has been much easier for me to work reskilling myself and redesigning my life with my boys, versus thinking about having to go back into a way of life that would make my heart pound with anxiety.

Just the thought of going back to my past life motivates me enough to keep plowing forward using my imaginary machete to cut down the high weeds, creating a new path. I love growth, the excitement of change, and the knowledge that I am rebuilding my self-esteem, eliminating my limiting beliefs, strengthening my decision-making abilities, and trusting in myself again.

I have to be honest and say that at the time that I am writing this chapter, my life is still changing. I have yet to find that financial abundance, as I would like it to be. It is the final link to my journey and I am still uncomfortable about that. I can honestly say that so far in this journey, I have been resilient in tapping into those very skill sets that *just don't translate.*

I am the happiest I have ever been. Truth be told, there are still many things I am working through that, as I learn, I apply, and I am in the best spot to be doing that. I have taken charge of my life. I regained my self-determination that I am enough and I can do this on my own. By my own, I mean with all the village and community that I have been cultivating and all the resources I have been tapping into.

There is a saying that I wish to bestow on to you. I have no idea where it came from, but it goes like this.

A closed mouth never gets fed. ~ Unknown

This means to ask for help. Seek out guidance, find mentors, confidants, safe people who you can trust with what's in your heart, trust with your worries, invest money in yourself to get help if needed or to also help reskill yourself, ask for financial assistance if you need it.

If I had to give advice to anyone who would like to be or is already in the middle of a life transition, I would say, you are not bothering people by asking for help. Those who love you and genuinely care for you would prefer you ask for help versus suffering in silence alone. They will get upset that you didn't ask them, and it is not your place to tell them they should not help you when they make an offer. Don't think for a minute that anyone in the world hasn't, at one time, asked for help to get them back on their feet. We all have, and we all should be asking for help. We are humans and we need to be connected. Never give up.

Najia Said

"There is no such thing as failure, only new opportunities presenting themselves to encourage you to make another decision." ~ Najia Said

In 2021, Najia faced a major cross road in her life. She either needed to go back to the continued disappointment of a traditional lifestyle lacking work life balance or get out of her own way to redesign a life that was more conducive for her and her two boys.

As a newly single mom, that was the monster that had been chasing her for years and now it was looking her dead in the eyes. Najia took a leap of faith and decided her best bet was to bet on herself. Instead of wallowing in self-doubt and pity, she dug in deep and faced her demons head-on once and for all. And thus began her journey of personal reinvention and discovery.

Having a diverse background and working an unconventional career in construction, Najia understands well the struggles many women face both inside and outside the home. One of Najia's best attributes is working with women who seek to reclaim who they are or who they want to be, while inspiring women to start taking action and ownership of their destiny. She provides a perspective on life that lends itself to personal empowerment.

Najia currently is an aspiring entrepreneur and homeschool mother.

Connect with Najia at https://www.linkedin.com/in/najiasaid/.

CHAPTER 18

From Vision to Victory

Sally Katherine Ross

How many times in your life have you given up on a dream? Everyone I know, at some point in their lives, has given up on a dream they've had. Often, expectations placed on us from society cause us to abandon our desires in order to be of service to others. Sometimes we give up out of fear of failure or even fear of success. Are you currently facing difficulties so great that you feel driven to abandon a goal? Have you lost the vision of your dream being possible? Do the roadblocks and challenges seem too overwhelming?

Take a moment and allow yourself to just breathe and relax. Think about how many times you committed yourself and achieved a major goal. Remember when you followed through with something that deeply inspired and motivated you. What wonderful events and people have entered your life as a result of your decision to persevere in all of those times? You have accomplished a great number of goals in your life and you should feel immensely proud.

Your life would be quite different if you had always given up every time life's challenges blocked your path, wouldn't it? This is why it is *imperative* that you stay on the path you have chosen, once you are absolutely convinced that it is the right path for you. Please note the key words: *absolutely convinced.* You might be feeling unsure as to whether you are on the right path. You may doubt your choices and question your own desires. The only person who can confirm if you are on the right path is *yourself.*

You must look deep inside yourself and listen for that inner voice. If there were absolutely no obstacle or hindrance keeping you from this goal, what would it look like? How would it feel? When you allow your conscious mind to connect with your body, your transformation has begun.

Here is how my journey began: from my childhood, dance and music have been my inspiration for living and my motivation to continually learn about the arts. Becoming a ballerina was my only wish from an early age. It took years of daily lessons, sore muscles, and bloody toes. The competition was immense, but I was my worst critic as I strived for perfection. However, every dancer knows *perfect* is unattainable. However, the eternal quest to improve my artistry and technique proved to be an excellent foundation for my dedication to my goals throughout my life.

Having become a ballerina, it was extremely satisfying to travel the world dancing professionally. Feeling blessed to have experienced those travels, my full immersion into international cultures taught me a great deal through their fascinating histories and traditions.

While living in Italy for seven years, I enjoyed dancing on stage and screen during my beautiful deep-dive into architecture, art, photography, and design. I even fell in love. After returning to America, my husband and I developed and ran several successful businesses together. Our beautiful hair salon provided a showcase for his talents as a hair stylist and makeup artist. Photo sessions and hair shows were part of the many artistic projects that we worked on together. We started a family and I experienced my dreams coming true. Raising our wonderful daughter filled my heart with complete bliss. Eventually, when time allowed me to dance again, I became a professional Flamenco dancer. My soul soared with joy as I danced with such expressive passion. Feeling on top of the world, I believed my future was dependable and secure.

However, a few years ago my world was turned upside down. Three major life transitions shook me for years and tossed me into an emotional abyss. Being laid off from a successful design job, my divorce and my mother's illness tore my entire family apart. Occurring within three-months of each other, these traumatic events nearly knocked me off of the deep end.

Although I believe that life's events have purpose and lessons for us to learn from, feelings of overwhelm made my life's challenges almost unbearable. Surrendering to victimhood and a lack mentality, I believed that all of my dreams for the future were impossible.

For several years I felt lost and without direction. It was a rocky, cluttered road that had me emotionally paralyzed by fear. No longer aligned with my true essence, my passions for art and design no longer brought me joy.

The circumstances I had found myself in left me feeling numb and empty. The lack of direction and purpose had caused the loss of my identity and sense of self-worth. Ready to resign myself to whatever life brought me, I was eager to blame my misfortune on destiny, as another unfortunate victim of circumstance. At the time, I was not aware how the loss of certain aspects of my life would have such a profound effect on my happiness and joy of living. I didn't see how my self-esteem had been so dependent on the roles that I had chosen or had been drawn to.

My roles in life had either been stripped away from me completely or had been transformed beyond recognition.

Feelings of worthlessness crushed the feelings of gratitude and self-confidence I once had. Since I was no longer needed as a spouse or employee, my thoughts of no longer having any value in society began to crush what remained of my sense of self. Decisions were made out of fear and I could not focus on progress.

Continuing on a downward spiral of self-doubt and self-sabotage, my life deteriorated even more. Eventually, late one night, I crumbled to the ground shaking and sobbing, "What am I going to do? How can I feel happy again?"

That was when I realized that I needed to make major changes in my life. Finally aware that I had to choose between staying gripped by fear and pain OR taking action to find a way to find myself again, I realized that I could *choose happiness*. I accept responsibility for living my life on my own terms and deserve to find joy and fulfillment.

It was a struggle to stay focused on changing my mindset. Making such huge shifts in my beliefs and habits proved extremely challenging. Frequent memories of traumatic events would haunt me and there were moments of extreme sadness and despair.

My love for my daughter gave me the motivation to keep going and the determination to stay strong and look for hope. She has inspired me her entire life. As a young adult, she traveled extensively around the nation and abroad. Her bravery and zest for life inspired me to search for what *would bring me joy*.

She reminded me of my twenty something self, when I first set off to explore the world. Wanting to be completely alive again, vibrant, and courageous, I knew I needed to stay on my path to find happiness. It became clear that if I gave up on my transformational journey, I couldn't be a source of positive energy for my daughter with her own life challenges.

Giving up on my growth would have denied us wonderful moments together sharing our life experiences, lessons, and observations. I wanted to inspire and encourage her on her own journey. It was worth continuing on my path, because we now have beautiful memories of sharing time, experiences, and laughter together.

So, I made myself a plan of action, which included a combination of help from others, self-discovery, and education. Medical professionals assured me that I was on the right track. By learning innovative healing modalities, I discovered how negative thoughts hold us captive in paradigms. I was then able to rid myself of limiting beliefs, negative self-talk, and other self-criticisms.

Besides my daughter, my biggest supporters were my coaches. Life coaches helped me explore self-nurturing tools that brought me a new sense of confidence. My business coach helped me discover a renewed sense of purpose for my business and a life mission that inspires and motivates me every day.

Creative projects and artistic endeavors helped me figure out what makes me happy and lights me up inside. They opened my mind and allowed me to pursue my passions again for art, design, and dance. My own dedication and persistence in taking action propelled me to follow through with my plan of action which delivered my transformation.

The KEY to never giving up on your dreams is to carry inside yourself, in every waking moment, a vision of that perfect life you desire. Let that vision evoke emotions. What will it feel like when you have accomplished your goal? Hold on to those feelings and recall them when you doubt yourself. This will inspire your choices that will take you to the next step. Sometimes we are not even able to imagine what we want, because we become trapped in paradigms and false beliefs. We are thrown into a state of reaction, of survival.

This is when we need to stop everything, take a moment to just be very still, and calm ourselves. By focusing on controlled deep breathing, our nervous system slows down and we feel centered enough to see what small steps we can take to feel better. Meditation and dance helped calm my anxiety and grounded me. Reflection and controlled breathing soothes you while movement releases the tension.

On May 2, 2019, the American Psychological Association published the results of a study developed by Nur Hani Zainal, MS, and Michelle G .Newman, PhD. Conducted over the course of eighteen years, the study of thousands of Americans showed that people who keep a positive outlook on life and strive to not give up on achieving their goals have less anxiety and depression. They also reported fewer panic attacks.

> *Clinicians can help their clients understand the vicious cycle caused by giving up on professional and personal aspirations. Giving up may offer temporary emotional relief but can increase the risk of setbacks as regret and disappointment set in. Boosting a patient's optimism and resilience by committing to specific courses of actions to make dreams come to full fruition despite obstacles can generate more positive moods and a sense of purpose.*
> ~ Nur Hani Zainal, MS

They discovered how persistence helps you achieve your dreams, **plus** the numerous mental health benefits you obtain by pursuing your goals.

Seeking the supervision of a medical professional is a priority. Wellness exams and good nutrition can greatly impact your well-being and quality of life. If feelings of depression are keeping you from enjoying life, be sure to ask for help. Major challenges in life can cause emotional tornadoes that you may not even be aware of.

My coaching uses several modalities, including physical movement. Dance movements facilitate my clients' transformation. The flow of energy, both physical and emotional, improves muscle strength, function, and flexibility while you process and transmute emotions that keep you feeling *stuck*. This results in better balance and stability, while feeling the joy and tranquility you greatly deserve!

Moving your body while feeling strong emotions helps you release tension. Using your conscious mind to tell your body to do something specific while you are feeling stress or anxiety is scientifically proven to calm your nerves. Athletes, performers, and business owners use coaches to improve their skills and help achieve their dreams. Discovering that goal setting is a huge factor in their success, they learned that coaches were crucial for their desired results. Grateful to their coaches for holding them accountable, they also credit *themselves* for making the commitment to never give up. Any life altering goal needs your commitment to your desired results. A coach that you trust can guide you.

You MUST pursue your passions. Human beings are gifted with creativity and imagination. If you have assembled a puzzle, you are creative. Finding solutions to everyday challenges takes imagination. We use them both in artistic and athletic activities. Using our senses, we make decisions according to what we think might happen and create in our minds an image of our desired result. The more we utilize these gifts through our passions, the more we nurture, stimulate, and strengthen our abilities.

Life is not always predictable, but there are countless activities and choices that we can be pretty sure about the outcome. Having a set plan for achieving your goals helps you establish a bit of control over events that are predictable. Since stress can happen to you when you don't expect it, even having a to-do list to follow or an activity to participate in can keep your brain focused and in control of at least some aspects of your life. This reduces stress and keeps you on track.

Having a routine is good for development and health
~ Dr. Kerry Ressler, Professor of Psychiatry at
Harvard Medical School

An enormous step that helped my transformation was behavior modification. Having always felt shy and uncomfortable in social situations, I designed a plan that showed how my new persona needs to be confident and outgoing. The plan included challenging myself with specific goals to find that confident woman inside me, yearning to be free!

Another factor that has contributed to my new identity is having made immense changes in my living environment. While unpacking hundreds of boxes after my move-in, I edited out what did not serve me anymore and only kept what I could use and/or what brought me joy. Actually, this physical activity also served as emotional healing: I learned how to edit out thoughts that I realized no longer served me and replaced them with encouraging affirmations. The activity held my focus and kept me from depression. Eventually, my coaches helped me learn how to look at painful memories in order to discover the source of the pain and negative thoughts in order to begin to heal and thrive.

By designing a step-by-step plan, I actually began to take on the behavior and characteristics of the woman I dreamed I could be. This actually redesigned my personality and my reality. Newly found courage enabled me to rediscover my authentic self.

Immensely grateful to be living in a new community with nurturing friendships, I am doing wonderful things that I never even dreamed of having the courage to do. This self-awareness allows me more freedom, strength, and confidence in my decisions. My life is better than I could ever have imagined.

Creativity and productivity both increased, as I upleveled my self-image. Through my system of goals and challenges, I gained confidence to dare myself to step out of the box. I redesigned a life that has given me more success, joy, and enduring friendships than ever before. Now, I dance in public like nobody is looking!

My transformational journey has been so powerful to me and inspired my coaching programs that are designed to help women who desire more abundance, confidence and joy in their lives and businesses. By redesigning your self-identity, you can actually create a new reality for yourself. Utilizing a combination of modalities, you can transform your life. Make the decision to uplevel your mindset and behavior to shift how you feel, then observe how your own superpowers make you your own hero!

Allow into your life only what inspires you and leave out any negative remnant from the past. Day by day, week by week, allow yourself to explore the thoughts and behavior of the YOU that you want to be. This will encourage your personal growth for your entire life.

This is a journey, not a sprint. Dedicate your time and energy to self-love through your commitment to follow your dreams. Others treat you in a way that directly correlates to how you feel about yourself. If you want to be respected and appreciated, you need to respect and appreciate who you are!

Allow yourself to explore creative and artistic activities, even if you feel that you lack the talent or skill. Learn to sing, dance, or play an instrument. Try a new sport or add to one that you've done here and there.

Create a feeling of comfort or elegance by designing your living areas that reflect who you want to become and how you want to feel. Rid yourself of anything that evokes negative feelings in you. This will open inner space for a continuous upward cycle of insights, self-nurturing beliefs, and beneficial behaviors. As it contributes to your personal growth and happiness, you can thrive and achieve your greatest dreams.

In Summary, never giving up will enlighten you to the amazing person you are. You will continuously notice and eliminate your limiting beliefs while learning to shift away from behaviors that work against your personal growth. By making changes in your mindset you will find many opportunities to improve your life. With stress diminished, you are able to navigate your emotions more easily.

1. Find coaches and mentors that can guide you through your journey.
2. Calm your anxiety through relaxation and meditation to look inward for inspiration.
3. Design a living environment that reflects your future self and desired feelings.
4. Self-Care includes exercise, healthy eating habits, and being grateful, kind, and forgiving to yourself, as well as others.
5. Pursue your passions, such as music, movement, sports, and art.
6. Become aware of behavior patterns that are keeping you stuck in negativity and shift your behavior to express a positive attitude towards life.

YOU can find confidence, strength, and courage which will result in more success and excitement in your life. You deserve it, and I believe that you also have the inner power to overcome life's challenges and setbacks. It begins with the *choice* to bring infinite joy and passion into your life. My journey continues and I am grateful that today I might open a door of possibility for you.

Sally Katherine Ross

Entrepreneur and author, Sally Ross, focuses on coaching women in transition to overcome life's challenges and gain courage so they can express their true essence and talents to the world. By rediscovering their true identity, they witness their own capabilities, imagination, and creativity.

Sally's custom programs help women committed to generating more success, abundance, and joy. Using timeless and proven healing modalities, her holistic and transformational coaching empowers women to feel more self-sufficient in business and relationships. Gaining inner strength and confidence, they redesign their personal image and manifest a future they desire:

- Remove emotional blocks and gain self-esteem.
- Learn to love every aspect of yourself.
- Envision and design a bold new persona.
- Challenge yourself to overcome fears.
- Feel confident to make choices reflecting a future of your own design.

Sally shares decades of insight and inspiration from her own challenges and victories. She instantly connects with clients with her motivational and innovative style. Sally believes that when women find true inner strength, regain self-confidence, and take action to uplevel their lives, they become unstoppable. Their lives become unforgettable.

Motivated by her own transformation, Sally helps women in transition build self-esteem, gain courage, and trust their inner voice so they can feel free, abundant, and authentic.

Connect with Sally at www.lifestyledesignmakeover.com.

CHAPTER 19

Operation Kick Cancer in the @$$!

Susan O. Beam

You can't wait until life isn't hard anymore
until you decide to be happy.
~Jane Marczewski, singer known as Nightbirde

It was the morning of October 26, 2011. I was sitting in the doctor's office, waiting for my test results. I can clearly remember the clock reading 9:35 and tears rolling down my face. They were five minutes late, and I was waiting to hear the results of my breast biopsy.

Let's back up for a moment. I had my routine *female* exam, including a mammogram, on Wednesday, October 12, 2011. I remember seeing a cartoon in the mammography room that said: "Mammographers are like magicians, they turn your cups into saucers!" I just laughed, as humor is such a big part of how I deal with life, especially difficult moments.

Five days later, I was notified by the radiologist's office that there was a *questionable abnormality* in the left breast image that needed further evaluation. After I received this notification, I called my mother and told her that I had to get more films done, because they found a questionable abnormality on my mammogram films. She promptly told me not to worry about this, because lots of people had to go back for repeat films. She also told me that everything would be fine and that she loved me.

I went to have the repeat films done on Thursday, October 20, 2011. I knew the mammogram technologist, so I just cried when I walked in the mammography room. The technologist was so sweet to me and did her best to comfort me as she was taking the necessary images of my left breast. She explained everything that she was doing, as she was taking the images. Once she was finished, she said that the *suspicious area* could still be seen. The next step was to go over to ultrasound and have an ultrasound done on my left breast. I remember texting my boss and telling her "Hi Ho, Hi Ho – it's off to ultrasound I go!" Needless to say, I was scared to death. The ultrasound couldn't tell exactly what this area was, so I was scheduled for a needle guided ultrasound biopsy of my left breast the next day.

The pathology report wouldn't be available for three business days. My husband and I were given an appointment to return to the office on Wednesday, October 26, 2011, for the results. These were the longest five days of my life!

While waiting for the biopsy results, I decided to prepare myself, mentally, for a positive biopsy result. I figured that it would be easier to accept a diagnosis of breast cancer, if I had mentally prepared for that result, rather than just blowing off the chances of me having a positive diagnosis for breast cancer. This was just another way I dealt with this situation.

Finally, the day of our appointment arrived. The appointment time was 9:30 a.m. on Wednesday, October 26, 2011. We arrived at the office and checked in. We were told to have a seat in the waiting room. When the minute hand of the clock on the wall moved to the 7, I began to cry. They were five minutes late for my appointment. The stress of waiting for the results came out in the tears that were running down my face. Finally, we were taken to an office where we got the results. The biopsy showed that I was positive for *infiltrating ductal carcinoma*. In plain English, I was told those three words no one wants to hear – "You have cancer." I was literally numb after hearing this diagnosis. I just cried in my husband's arms. I prayed that God would lead me down the right path to the necessary treatment for this disease.

When Stuart and I went back to our various places of employment, Stuart heard a song on the radio. He thought it was a song about the journey we were about to endure. He heard the same song, later that afternoon, on his way home from work. He called the radio station to find out what the song was. It turned out to be *I'm Gonna Love You Through It* by Martina McBride. Stuart bought me the album and I listened to the song and just cried as I heard the words. This, in fact, was our story and Stuart said he'd be there to love me through it – just as the song stated.

The next day, I was scheduled for an appointment at the Breast Clinic. I met with a surgeon, radiation oncologist, and medical oncologist to discuss my treatment options. The very first step of this process was genetic testing. I needed to see if I was positive or negative for the breast cancer genes known as BRCA1 and BRCA2. I had the genetic testing done on Friday, October 28. 2011. The results of the genetic testing would help to determine what kind of surgical intervention would be needed. The results of the genetic testing would take about ten days. I had appointments scheduled for November 14 and on November 17. I would meet with the medical oncologist, to find out the results of my genetic testing on the first date and I would meet with the surgeon on the second date.

I was nervous about getting the results of the genetic testing back. If my BRCA1 and BRCA2 genes came back positive, I would have to have a more invasive surgery, as I would need to have my uterus and ovaries taken out. Thank God, the genetic testing was negative.

I had an appointment with the first surgeon on November 17. He said, due to the small size of the tumor, I would probably have a lumpectomy and a sentinel lymph node biopsy. I had a second opinion, with a different surgeon on November 18. The second surgeon is a big Carolina Tarheels fan. I am a big Duke University fan. These two teams are major rivals. Knowing this and utilizing my humor, I told the doctor that I had "A Tarheel tumor that needed to be healed!" He just looked at me and laughed.

I also had to explain to him how Duke, Carolina, and Breast Cancer were all related. You see: If you take a piece of paper and put the Duke mascot on the left side and the Tarheel mascot on the right side. Then, you title the page "Basic Math" and put a > (greater than sign) sign between the two mascots. Thus: BASIC MATH Blue Devils > Tarheels.

Now, you will notice that the Tarheels are on the RIGHT side. Let's put this into perspective with my breast cancer. Now, take that same piece of paper and hold it up to your chest. Guess what happened?

Duke is now on the RIGHT side, the breast without cancer, and Carolina is on the LEFT side, the breast with cancer.

In other words, the Carolina breast is the diseased one and it needs to BE HEELED and that is why I am having a lumpectomy, so I can BE HEALED!

He agreed that I would probably just need the procedures, as discussed by the first surgeon. Once the surgery was completed and the tissue samples were sent to pathology, a treatment plan would be determined – based on the results of the surgical biopsy.

In the mix of all this stuff, we ,as a family, had planned to go on a Disney Cruise to celebrate my parents' 50th Anniversary in

December of 2011. I was so scared that I wouldn't be able to go. Later, I was thrilled to learn that I was able to go on this cruise. I had already decided that I wasn't going to let a little BS (boob surgery) keep me from going on this family cruise.

The American Cancer Society has a flagship fundraising event called Relay For Life. I signed up for this event, in November of 2011, as a SURVIVOR. Relay For Life events love to celebrate their survivors. This is another one of my coping mechanisms, to always take time to celebrate various milestones that you reach in life. The day before my surgery, I received a card from my work family. It said: "No Ocean can hold it back. No river can overtake it. No whirlwind can go faster. No army can defeat it. No law can stop it. No distance can slow it. No disease can cripple it. No force on earth is more powerful or effective than THE POWER OF PRAYER!"

Faith is another avenue that helps me through difficult times. I was never afraid to tell someone about my diagnosis of breast cancer. I figured that the more people that knew, the more people that could pray for me and I had A LOT of prayer warriors!

Well, the morning of my surgery finally arrived. I was a nervous wreck, to say the least. I had to be at the hospital at 6:30 a.m. on December 9, 2011. The nursing staff was so friendly and provided the most amazing care. My nurse even took the time to pray with me, before I left for my pre-surgical procedures. I was deeply touched by this act of kindness, as our minister had not arrived by the time I left the Same Day Surgical Unit.

I had to have a sentinel node biopsy and a needle localization procedure. The first procedure was to inject radioactive dye in the lymph system, so they could tell which lymph nodes were hot and needed to be removed during the surgical procedure. After the eight injections were completed, the Physician Assistant that did that procedure said the breast needed to be massaged to get the dye moving within the lymphatic system.

I joked with the male PA and said "What, you are not going to finish providing the excellent care that you started?"

The look on his face was priceless! I just told him that my husband was waiting just outside the procedure room and to please get him.

Having fun and joking around, despite the circumstances, is yet another coping mechanism that I use to get through difficult situations. It really is true that attitude is half the battle!

After the sentinel node biopsy, I had to have a needle localization procedure. This is a procedure that places a needle in the location of the tumor, so that the surgeon knows where to go and remove it. To get ready for this procedure, I had to have my left breast placed in the mammography machine and squashed to death! The radiologist came into the room, and he was over my left shoulder. I had him navigate between myself and the breast gripping device so that I could (somewhat) comfortably see him as he was explaining what he was going to do. I brought two stress toys with me to this procedure. The first was a football, because I was about to have a ball. The second was a port-a-john, as things were about to really get deep!

When the radiologist finished placing the needle in my breast, I had a Styrofoam cup placed over the needle, so that I wouldn't accidentally dislodge it. I looked really sexy, with that cup under my hospital gown!

Once the procedures, in radiology, were completed, I had to go to the radiology holding area as they weren't quite ready for me in surgery. We met up with our minister. It was a great comfort to have Pastor Mike there, praying for me before surgery. Our church was in between pastors, so we asked Pastor Mike to be with us as we prepared for my surgery.

When they were ready to take me to the surgery holding areas, I was able to kiss Stuart good-bye and I was then wheeled off to surgery.

When I arrived in the surgical suite, I had to pee, again! I remember thinking that I hadn't had anything to eat or drink since midnight – why was I having to pee so much? The nurse told me that it was just nerves. Once I got settled, my medical team introduced themselves to me. I met my nurses, the anesthesia team, and I saw my surgeon. I remember telling them I didn't want any happy drugs prior to going to the operating room. I shared that I would like to know exactly where I am going and be moved onto the operating table, before any pre-op meds are given.

When I saw my surgeon, I gave him a hug. His shoulder hit my right hand and dislodged the IV (intravenous drip). I told him that he just messed up my IV. He said, he didn't mess up my IV, I messed up my IV. Anyway, the CRNA had to restart the IV so I could receive the meds needed for the surgical procedure. I had the nurses laughing, while I was insisting it was the surgeon that messed up my IV. Truth be known, at least the IV was dislodged and not the needle that was in my left breast!

I remember going to OR 7 (Operating Room 7). Once in the room, I was asked to move from the stretcher to the table. They hooked all the various devices needed for surgery. The next thing I knew, I was waking up in the Recovery Room and the surgery was over! Once I was stable, I was sent back to the Day Surgery Unit to finish recovering and then we were discharged home. We went to eat seafood and I proudly wore my Mickey Mouse pajamas into the restaurant.

I had my surgery on Friday morning. Stuart and I went to church on Sunday and boy, were people surprised to see us! Yes, I wasn't letting a little BS (boob surgery) keep me from going to church.

The week following surgery was busy as well. I had to go to the surgeon's office on Monday, as the surgical drain quit working. Since everything looked so good, the surgeon went ahead and pulled out the drain. It was such a relief to have that drain gone!! Stuart's aunt visited us on Tuesday. My boss brought us lunch, from Chick-fil-A on Wednesday. It felt so good to visit my place of work, when I didn't have to do anything work related! I had my first official post-op visit on Thursday. The surgeon said everything was looking fine and that I was cleared to go on our Disney Cruise on December 18, 2011. Score one for being on the way to kicking cancer in the @$$! Due to the healing incisions, I just couldn't go into the ocean. I took it a step further and decided not to go swimming at all. The surgeon also told me that everything regarding my pathology report looked good, but he didn't have the final report. I also found out I would be meeting with the medical oncologist on January 5, 2012.

Another strategy I used was to write the word CANCER on a piece of paper. I gave the piece of paper to my friend, Melissa, to hold while we were gone on our cruise – so I didn't have to worry about cancer while I was on vacation.

So, I went to my medical oncology appointment and found out that I had a very small tumor. In fact, it was 1.1 cm in size. I was staged at a Stage 1, as my cancer was caught very early. I am living proof that EARLY DETECTION SAVES LIVES!

I also found out that I was *triple positive* for the kind of cancer I had. This means that my tumor was ER+ (estrogen receptor), PR+ (progesterone receptor), and HER2+. HER2+ breast cancers are typically more aggressive, so I had to have four rounds of chemotherapy. I had a targeted therapy, called Herceptin, to treat the HER2+ part of the cancer. I also had to have radiation therapy and hormone therapy. All these treatments were done in hopes of preventing the recurrence of breast cancer.

I decided to name my cancer journey Operation Kick Cancer in the @$$! There were five phases of this journey.

Phase 1: The lumpectomy and sentinel node biopsy (completed on December 9, 2011).

Phase 2: Port placement and chemotherapy. The surgeon said my veins wouldn't tolerate the harsh chemo drugs, so I had a port placed prior to beginning chemo.

Phase 3: Herceptin, which was given via IV every three weeks for a year.

Phase 4: Radiation Therapy which consisted of 36 treatments, five days a week.

Phase 5: Tamoxifen which turned into Arimidex, as I couldn't take the Tamoxifen due to another medication I was taking. I also had to have a monthly injection of Eligard. This phase was the longest phase as it started in July 2012 and finished in July 2022. Yes, I was on the 10-year plan due to the fact that I was diagnosed at an early age. I was 44 at the time of diagnosis.

In closing, I would like to remind people to always celebrate milestones along the way. Stuart and I went out to dinner or took a cruise to celebrate the different milestones that were completed during my treatment. It's also OK to vent through writing. There was one day I was really frustrated, so I wrote this poem:

What if Dr. Suess Had Cancer?

I have cancer, yes, I do.It's not in my top or bottom or crest.
Rather, this damn cancer is in my breast.
Surgery was a must,
so that the cancer will bite the dust!
After surgery, test results reveal
Stage One, ER +, PR +, and + for HER2+ as well ...
HER2+ breast cancers tend to be more aggressive,
so my oncologist makes my treatment most impressive ...
Four rounds of chemo (every three weeks you see)
then a drug called Herceptin will be given for a year ...
followed by Radiation Therapy, oh my ...
which will make my boob tanner than my thigh ...

Also, take time to journal throughout your journey. I utilized Caring Bridge for that purpose. Also, remember that NO ONE FIGHTS ALONE and that THE "C" IN CHRIST IS FAR BIGGER THAT THE "c" in cancer.

Susan O. Beam

Susan O. Beam is a true inspiration and champion when it comes to "Never Giving Up." She fought tirelessly for ten years against cancer, experiencing many scares and potential life altering circumstances. With her loving husband, Stuart by her side, she faced each challenge and used it as a catalyst for helping others. Her journey with cancer taught her the value of life and she chose to allow this experience to help others. Susan's entrepreneurial journey in offering higher quality at lower cost healthcare options has empowered people to take control of their healthcare and take back their life as a result. Through this journey, Susan has become the voice of hope for people during times of crisis, showing us all the power to "Never Give Up."

Connect with Susan at: www.susanobeam.acnibo.com.

CHAPTER 20

She Has Always Been Here

Susannah Dawn

I'm not what I used to be, yet I am who I've always been. ~ Susannah Dawn

"That's not who you are!"

Visualize being told those words by a parent, feel the negative emotional sentiment contained in each syllable, and realize you were seven years old. Imagine what it must feel like to be rejected for who you are by those who are supposed to raise you ... protect you ... be your role models and support you growing up.

It happened to me.

The instant I was on the receiving end of the first spanking associated with my dad's reaction towards my true self, was also the onset of my emotional decline. It was the moment when I withdrew from family ... friends ... the rest of society. As a seven-year-old child, suddenly, no place felt safe in this world.

Thereafter, for most of my life, I hid myself. Any relationships in my life were limited to superficial conversations. Somehow, I understood that the friendships I needed – I yearned for – in my life … were not possible. You know the ones where friends become so close, they can almost finish each other's sentences. Each knows what the other person likes, as well as to what lengths they are willing to go to avoid what they dislike.

These are friends who aren't just family … they are closer than siblings and would do anything for each other.

Such relationships were no longer an option for me. To be close to anyone became difficult, as it required me to let down my guard, to dismantle a wall I had quickly built around myself for my own safety. Once begun, I spent years carefully adding to this wall, brick by brick, block by block, to keep out those who would harm me in any way. Its design had one purpose: to insulate me from the rejection I felt from that early age, which began with my father and continued well past high school.

At this point, there is something you should know about me. Understand, this aspect doesn't define who I am. However, it had the potential to play a significant role in how others would view me once – if – they found out… and it was likely to be a negative disposition.

If you were to look at me now, the face you would see is only three years old. I was treated as a boy from birth because that was the shell into which I was born. However, from the age of three, I knew I was a girl. I vividly remember going to bed at night, praying to God to let me wake up a girl. I never told anyone … the idea of doing so was never in my mind. I just knew who I was.

Even before my dad's actions, I knew enough to try to keep that part of me hidden to avoid being teased by classmates. During the dance section of PE, where the boys outnumbered the girls, I was picked to be with the girls to even the numbers. Inside, this elated me to no end! However, I also knew I had to feign not enjoying it to avoid being teased. Also, my best and closest friends were girls, and we did everything together, including getting into trouble a time or two in school. We were inseparable.

Yet something happened between second and third grade, thereby laying the foundation for that solid wall I built. It was the moment my dad caught me trying on my mom's clothes. It was the day he began to take drastic steps to eradicate who I was and focused on molding me into who – what – he wanted … expected.

Looking back on the period of world history when I grew up, and knowing how things were when my dad was young, his actions would be applauded by most of society. The spanking I received was designed to knock from my mind any thoughts of doing such a thing again … designed to correct my thinking into accepting that I was what he said I was: a boy.

Before you try to chalk this up as another trans story, consider this: women who are neurodiverse, overcame addictions, have a non-local regional accent, and so many other labels we deal with, could have similar stories and experiences in their lives.

That initial spanking was only the first sign of being rejected by my own dad. My sense of rejection was supported by a few more spankings, until I became good at hiding who I was. Additional negative reinforcement came through his verbal comments through teasing and ridicule, especially if I did anything that might be considered girlish.

I always wore my pants at my waist … my dad told me to lower them as they were too high. I didn't understand why he cared, especially as the length was proper. To me, having them sit at my waist was natural … although it also turned out to be where girls wore their pants.

When I played with action figures, he always commented about me playing with dolls. His tone and words implied that what I enjoyed was a bad thing, since only girls played with dolls. Never mind that he and mom got me a toy camper and associated figure one Christmas. It was almost like he bought them with the intent of making me feel silly or wanted to shame me for playing with something that only girls played with, all in the name of fixing me.

Each physical and verbal abuse from my dad only strengthened my walls, thickened them to close off my heart from getting hurt anymore. At the same time, I had been emotionally abused. Even though there was something different about me, there was no one available for me to talk with, to help me understand why I was different than other kids.

By the time I arrived at middle school, I had no friends and no idea how to make any. Though I tried to play basketball with the boys, I quickly gave up as it wasn't fun. If I played four square, it was rare for me to get beyond the first square as the other kids formed partnerships with the goal of getting me out. I spent my time on the playground alone ... except when chased by the kid who bullied me. It all compounded into the sense of feeling unwanted wherever I went.

I felt trapped in a box from which I didn't know how to escape, with a growing sense of being an imposter.

The first box I had to deal with was living a life based on what was expected of me due to my shell, my body. I tried to live as others told me to be, tried to fit in with boys at school, with men in church, and even as a US Army Cavalry officer, yet nothing felt right. I knew I was female, yet family and society would not allow the authentic me to safely exist beyond the darkness found in my own box.

The only way I would be allowed to live – even if it were barely surviving, became crystal clear to me. I had to abide by the rules dictated towards me by others regarding who and what I was. It required hiding my authentic female self from those around me, something that negatively impacted my quality of life ... my ability to endure. I could only be Susannah in the confines of my home.

When we hide who we are because of fear, we allow ourselves to be trapped in a box where that same fear becomes our constant – and only – companion. We listen to the lies it tells us, lies with a few grains of truth woven throughout to make them credible … believable. We'll hide our authentic selves for fear of what might happen to us if anyone learned our truth. We presume that anyone we open up to will harm us physically, verbally, emotionally, or some combination of them all.

That led to a loss of self-confidence, and questioning if I could succeed in life while walking through it as an imposter. I knew I was a woman, that my soul was female, yet I had to pretend to be male. I had to keep my authentic self hidden from public view, behind that carefully built wall.

Again, consider someone who is dealing with imposter syndrome, has mental health issues, is LGBTQ+, or so many other reasons or labels identifying aspects a person would hide from the people around them so they could try to fit in. How much energy is wasted trying to keep the secret hidden and thereby holds them back from engaging with the people around them? I was wasting energy hiding myself from the world, feeling it suck away my life force while losing my self-esteem, self-confidence, and self-worth along the way.

Living a life based on what others expected and told me to be then created a sense of my feeling like a fraud in life, an imposter, which was why I dealt with Imposter Syndrome for most of my life. My imposter box was what I called a *Chameleon Imposter Syndrome Box*. It had a tendency to change and shift when it thought I was slipping from its grip.

For years I tried to identify as a boy, which made it all the more difficult to feel confident about my abilities … in myself. I was literally told to live my life in deceit – and to like it. That contributed to my feeling like a fraud … an imposter in my own skin, and in virtually every setting I was placed.

Imposter Syndrome then permeated into other areas of my life. Even with my success as an Army officer and in business, it was hard to believe I deserved them. I couldn't hear the truth if anyone told me I did well. My fears downplayed such comments as, "They're just being nice," "They don't realize how you screwed up _____," "You only got that role because _____," and so many other such thoughts that made sure any praise was dampened.

Imposter Syndrome also took its toll on me over the years by downplaying my authentic self. It kept me locked away by guaranteeing that, should I ever exit my dark closet and venture into the world, I would be ridiculed, likely hurt physically, and regret ever having stepped away from the safety of that dark space.

Often, when I look back on it all, I question how I ever survived to get to where I am today. Many times, I felt it would be far better for me to no longer exist than to be a burden to those around me. I had a now ex-spouse whose general comments during our marriage implied I was a drain to her. Since I had no desire to inconvenience others, I wished either someone else would enter her life and sweep her away to the life she deserved, or that something catastrophic would happen to me. I had a family who made it clear during general conversations that someone like me would not be accepted nor tolerated, so I knew it would be better to pass away than tell them my truth. Death felt better than living an un-authentic life.

Too many of us are told by family members, friends … even society … that we are only the person whom they view us as …. an opinion solely based on what our shell physically – biologically – looks like. They refuse to acknowledge our spirit … our soul, which was placed in these shells in which we walk the earth. Yet, it's our soul that is who we truly are, and which was placed here with a purpose and skillset unique to each of us to make the world better.

Though others may refuse the truth about our core being ... our soul, we understand who we are – who we were created to be – far beyond what anyone else could even imagine. We understand who we are better than those who cannot begin to identify with us or our situation ... and often don't want to.

Then, a door was opened that I thought would remain locked all my life. It had been almost 50 years since I first receded into that dark box at the age of seven, yet the door was being opened for me so that I could begin to step out into the world as who I was created to be ... Susannah.

In 2020, I began to emerge from a fifty-year hiatus. Over the next few years, that little girl I was back then, who was pushed aside in an attempt to eradicate her, re-emerged. I went through my own personal – and total – reinvention, taking the steps necessary to live as my authentic self. With each step on that journey, she slowly exited her box, in turn, filling me up with the joy and love I had been missing all my life. Something else that came with her was a return of my confidence, self-esteem, and self-worth. And though the journey wasn't easy, I didn't have to walk that path alone.

In the beginning, friends I never expected were placed in my path, each one filled with love and support. They never pushed me to come out any further than I was comfortable yet encouraged me to take every step that led to where I am today. I thank the Lord for each and every one of them. I trusted their words and encouragement, for they became true friends who supported me and were willing to be as open and honest with me as I was in telling them my story. They never saw me as a trans woman, only as the woman I have always been. That's why I knew I could never have survived, couldn't live as my authentic self beyond my front door in the beginning, without the wonderful support and love I received from the beautiful ladies who helped me spread my wings and fly those first couple of years.

That was followed by a new set of friends, and again, the vast majority being women. We connected on a business platform, yet our connections ran deeper than resumes and job searches. We opened up with each other about our own stories, our own backgrounds that we had previously feared telling anyone. Through sharing came a deepening closeness between us. When I told my story, all of them replied with love and support, saying how they only saw my authentic self ... Susannah.

It was a total affirmation, the acknowledgment by new friends, that I was coming across as my true self. It was freeing to realize I didn't have to hide in a box anymore, I didn't have to wear the heavy weight on my shoulders placed there by my fears. That was quickly followed by a simple, yet mind-blowing understanding: when I own my fear, my fear no longer controls me. Once I stood up to my fear, I gained full power and authority over it. That included the choice to tell whom I wanted that I was trans, which embraced the options to tell them my story when ... how ... where ... and IF I wanted. It also meant that, should someone find out and try to control me with the threat – the fear – of them telling others, it would no longer worry me as I wholeheartedly owned my story ... owned that which I feared ... and not the other way around.

Owning who I am ... who I've always been ... led to another understanding.

With all that happened in my life, the ups and downs ... the pains I endured in childhood and beyond, I'm often asked what I would change. People ask me what advice I'd give to avoid some of the pains I went through, so that others who relate to my story in their own ways might learn from my journey.

It's an interesting question, and I understand why people ask it. However, when I truthfully answer them, many seem confused. They usually wonder why I have such a simple answer ... with a deeper explanation.

The truth is, I wouldn't change a thing.

"How can that be?" they often ask, frequently with quizzical looks during video chats.

I let them know that, while I didn't like who I saw in the mirror for most of my life, I now love the person I've become. The face looking back is my authentic self, the woman I've always been, and she is beautiful.

It's why I believe in the *Butterfly Effect*, as described by Ray Bradbury in his short story, *A Sound of Thunder*. To go back in time and change even the tiniest thing, say, going back millions of years in the past and stepping on a single butterfly, would likely alter the present in unexpected ways. Should I change something in my past, maybe start my transition to become my authentic self sooner, or change a small decision I was regretting, I would become a different person … and quite possibly it would be someone I don't like. This is why I don't consider thoughts of changing my past, instead acknowledging, and forgiving what happened to me. By forgiving those who harmed me – including the times I realize it was me, I release the weight of the past that held me down to live in the light of the present. In this way, it's why I can say, "I'm not what I used to be, yet I am who I've always been."

By overcoming a past filled with pain and despair, to never give up when it was so easy to do just that, I'm able to live life to the fullest in the present. And as I said before, when I look in the mirror, I can finally be happy as I love the person looking back at me … I love who I am as my authentic self.

Susannah Dawn

Susannah Dawn entered 2022 with a total reinvention, and now looks at life and business from a vantage point set beyond labels … beyond boxes … those places in which our fears work hard to confine us, as they try to keep us from seeing how we are so much more than boxes and labels could ever express.

Susannah Dawn's experience in leadership roles spans a diverse group of industries, including U.S. Army Cavalry officer, construction management for design / build commercial projects, managing $20-$30-million-dollar energy efficiency programs, and writing for renewable energy firms (solar, wind, intertidal).

A motivational speaker, storyteller, and business consultant, Susannah Dawn no longer fits the proverbial box – and never did. She speaks at length on the importance of being our authentic selves and how to turn the obstacles of pivoting – of reinvention, into speed bumps. Susannah works with individuals, groups, and organizations as they consider their own reinvention processes so they, too, can move beyond boxes and labels.

Connect with Susannah at https://www.linkedin.com/in/susannah-dawn-freelance-writer/.

CHAPTER 21

Never Give Up – Single Parent

Teresa Dawn Johnson

When I was growing up, my parents were excellent role models of perseverance and determination. I did not realize until I was older how great an impact their influence had on me. In the 1980s, my parents would struggle with jobs. Some jobs ended. Companies folded. Our family would relocate out of state in hopes of finding stability and income. Then, unfortunately, at the place where my father worked, the union would go on strike and my family would move back and then it would happen again. Yes, my parents were unhappy about these things, but they got back up and kept on going.

So, for me as a parent of an autistic son and in a not-so-great marriage, I was not going to allow these obstacles to deter me from being able to do the best for my two sons, my spouse and myself. When my oldest son was not able to reach his age-appropriate milestones, we took Sean to speech, physical and occupational therapies. I would work with Sean at home with his speech therapy. When our second son, Nick was born, it became clear that there was more to my relationship with my spouse than I knew on the surface. Once these were addressed,

I began getting help for myself while my spouse got help for himself. I was so determined not to abandon my marriage that we had five separations over a six-year time period. Unfortunately, I could not continue staying in the marriage, but I would not give up on myself or my two sons.

While married, during times of separation and divorce, I continued working on me and my personal growth. I attended meetings for my codependent recovery, had a sponsor and worked the program. I was active in my church with service and in women's bible studies. I joined a local autism support group, where I served and gained knowledge to help my autistic son and our family.

The sole reason I persevered was through God and my faith. I showed my light to others, while those who worked through God, shined His light on me. During the journey, God gave me the strength to endure the obstacles.

I can do all things through Christ who strengthens me. ~Philippians 4:13

Autism diagnosis

One day in 1997, my spouse and I went to see the behavioral psychologist to have my son, Sean, evaluated. We parked the car in the Southern Illinois University School of Medicine's large parking garage and his dad carried Sean, while I led the way to the doctor's office. Sean was two years old, but was a new walker. He had just started walking at 22 months of age. It was easier to carry him, than let him walk. We had a long wait in the waiting room, which was large and accommodated many doctors. There were at least three check-in desks. There were several rocking toys and books for children. Sean wanted to see if he could get out all the magazines, as no one magazine interested him. The more we waited, the more agitated

Sean became. The more agitated Sean was, the more aggravated Justin and I were. Sean roamed all over the waiting area. He could not sit still. After about an hour and forty-five minutes, a nurse called for Sean.

The nurse directed us down the hallway to a small room where we met the female behavioral psychologist. She asked us questions about Sean. "How is his behavior at home? Does he whine a lot? What is he able to do? What does he spend most of his day doing?" Then, she interacted with Sean, to see what he would or would not do for her.

The psychologist would tell us her diagnosis and assessment in two weeks. We could not pick the date of the follow-up appointment and Justin had to work that day. I was told not to bring Sean, because the consultation would be to inform me of Sean's development.

When I returned to the clinic to see the psychologist, I noticed other children in the waiting room who acted much like Sean. I did not care how long I waited, but I did anticipate an answer to help Sean.

She asked me to sit down.

She said, "The first thing I want to tell you is that you have a very lovable, sweet boy. What I must tell you may be a bit hard to take. Your husband was not able to make it?"

"No," I said. "He was scheduled to work."

"My training in my expertise of behavior and assessing Sean, tells me that Sean is on the autism spectrum," she said.

"What does that mean?" I asked.

"In order to relate in a way you can understand, autism is a brain behavioral disorder that affects social behavior, as well as, the ability to learn the way you and I do," she said.

She continued to tell me more which just devastated me.

"Have you noticed, he doesn't point up to the sky and say, 'See Mommy, plane?' Why? Because he is in his own world," she said.

I did not understand what she meant.

"Your son will not know how to make friends. He will not ever have a girlfriend, get married and most certainly not have children. He may not be able to function, as an adult, on his own," she said.

The tears poured down my face. I could not stop crying.

I do not recall what she said after that. My thoughts just started racing. He is my only child. He is not even two years old. I instantly could not stand this doctor. I hated her. How dare she tell me that Sean had no future?

She gave me some handouts and a book list of recommended reading. The book list contained books on autism. She said the books would describe, in more detail, about this condition.

As I left her office, I became enraged at my spouse. He was not here to comfort me. I felt horrible. Could there be any hope for Sean? I was also angry at God. What purpose did He have in this? Could I be strong enough to take care of Sean?

I had recently gotten a job as a part-time librarian. I applied for the job on a whim, kind of hoping I would get it, but would not be devastated if I did not. So, I took that book list and proceeded to get online on the interlibrary loan to request three books on the book list.

I would check the bag every day to see if my requested books had come in. One book did come in on a Friday and our family was to go camping with my parents that weekend. I read as much as I could of that book while camping.

Unfortunately, nothing the book described was close to Sean's behavior. The book explained that people with autism did not like to be touched and had an extreme dislike for hugs. Sean loved hugs, in fact, my mother was known for rubbing Sean's stomach, while rocking him to sleep.

He played with toys, not creating imaginary play, as the books indicated. I did notice he liked playing by himself, but he did interact with his dad, me, and my parents very well. He smiled and for the most part, was a happy child.

I concluded that we had to get another diagnosis. I contacted our family doctor, who suggested that we take Sean to see a neurologist in our health insurance network. Dr. Dove was so nice. He examined Sean and did brain activity tests while Sean slept. Dr. Dove sent us to the lab to have Sean's urine collected and evaluated, which was an ordeal.

Dr. Dove sent us to St. Louis Children's Hospital for testing on Sean, as well as, questions about his dad's and my medical history. We discovered that Sean inherited his large head from his dad. His dad's head was larger than the average head size. No discoveries were made, but I still was not satisfied.

He said, in his opinion, Sean has pervasive developmental disorder which is identical to autism spectrum disorder. The main thing about the diagnosis is that it will help him get more services in school. More services will only enhance Sean's education, he said.

Our speech therapist recommended that we take Sean to be observed at the Speech and Hearing Clinic at Eastern Illinois University. I was comfortable going there. After all, it is where I earned my bachelor's degree. Two graduate students, under the instruction of a doctorate professor, played with and observed Sean.

They concluded that Sean had pervasive developmental disorder (PDD), but not autism spectrum disorder, as defined, because Sean was very social with the graduate students.

I had an inkling of hope, thinking okay Sean is delayed, but we can help him catch up. We will get him into preschool and the teachers will work their magic. I had been doing my part by taking him to speech and occupational therapy. His brain will click and everything will be right with the world.

Overtime, this was not the case. As time progressed and the school worked with Sean, it became evident that Sean did indeed have autism. I never gave up on Sean or on being a parent. I became involved with our local autism support group. I learned the tools necessary for us to have the services and the programs our family needed through the help of our local autism group. Those programs made it possible for Sean to have day services after he graduated high school.

Money tense situation

As a single parent, money can be a tense situation. I depended on the child support, my income and my autistic son's social security income. I have a bachelor's degree, but finding a good paying job was difficult. I worked clerical jobs and nothing paid well. Most of the clerical jobs were on temporary assignment. A woman of God at my church, who led our Sunday morning women's Sunday school class, had inadvertently become my mentor. Not only was she there for me through my marriage and then later, divorce, she advised me to call around to different insurance agencies in our state capital to see who had any openings. I did, and within a month I had an interview. Three months later, I was hired and started in the job.

I studied for my property and casualty license exam and passed. The agent where I had started ended her agency. Then, I ended up working in the same city where I live now. I am still there, eighteen years later. I did the work. I am grateful for the mentorship my friend gave me.

I also explored a professional networking group, Women in Communications, prior to working in insurance. I had been a student member in college. After one meeting, they encouraged me to speak with a publisher of a local business journal. The meeting went so well that I freelanced for the publication for fifteen years and it became a great additional income source and kept my skills up as a writer. I was able to freelance in conjunction with my day job. My true passion is writing. Whatever your true passion is, return to it. It is what you have been gifted to do. It is what lights your soul. Pursue your passion.

Bullying

As parents, we try our best, but our children have difficulties we are not in tune with. Somehow, as a parent, I found myself not paying full attention. My youngest son went through difficulty in his sixth-grade year, his first year at a large junior high school. He had mentioned to me that he wanted to be home schooled. I had to tell him that I could not see how that was possible, since I worked a full-time job and I had his autistic brother to take care of in the evenings. He said he did not like the junior high school, but I did not have a full picture of the situation.

It came to pass that my son had retaliated against bullying and had then been expelled. I did not want him to be in a school for delinquents, where he would be patted down and go through a metal detector. I would envision him being in a school with the students he was trying to avoid. I continually ask God for help and He puts people where they are called. A friend at my church knew a couple of people on the school board of a local Christian school. She told them the situation, we applied to be a part of the school and the Christian school board accepted our application.

It was everything that my youngest son needed. They would check on his mood in the morning and at the end of the school day. The classroom size was smaller and he got the teacher instruction attention he needed. He was accountable for late work and allowed to get organized. He stayed there for the next two and half years, graduated from there his eighth-grade year and went back to public school his freshman year in high school.

At the time, this was the most horrendous thing I had been through as a parent, even after my oldest son's autism diagnosis. All the obstacles along my path had become my path. The tuition for the school was an obstacle. I truly did not know how I was going to manage, but our family did. God provided a way. Somehow, I was able to manage our finances.

And my God will supply every need of yours
according to his riches in glory
in Christ Jesus. ~Philippians 4:19

Codependency

Prior to getting married, I was codependent and was unaware I had the characteristics of codependency. When choosing our life partner, we have a good understanding of why we choose them. You feel they have the same core values. You relate on several levels. You truly think you are a good match. My codependent characteristics were there prior to getting married, but surfaced more so during the marriage and needed to be addressed for myself. I am grateful that my former spouse and I were able to get help for ourselves, regardless of the outcome of our relationship.

I have spent many years in codependent recovery. There have been times in my life where I wanted to give up. Times where I did not know where I could go on. I wanted my relationship with my sons' father to work out so desperately. I would be at my bottom, wanting my spouse to be better. I did not want my life to be better until I, indeed, hit my bottom.

Twenty-three years ago, I went to my first codependent meeting so desperate to be well, to feel better, to stop the agony and the pain. I wanted to be happy. I wanted to stop having fights and arguments. It was not just my spouse, but other relationships. I did not even know there could be a better life. At my first meeting, when it was my time to share, I spoke through streams of tears. I do not even know what I said. I do know that I felt welcomed, listened to, and not judged. After the meeting, we talked more and for the first time, I felt hope.

There were people there who had been where I have been and they understood. They told me to keep coming back. So, I did.

After going to the meetings for over a year, I got a sponsor. I was quite stubborn. I thought I knew best. I thought I had all the answers. I needed to give up that type of thinking if I wanted to get well. I knew I needed a tough love sponsor. I picked the right one and she accepted. What I love about our codependency program is that it is a program that you can work at your own pace. If you want to be miserable, you can stay miserable. If you want to get better, get in there, do the work and you will see the results.

Things that I knew as head knowledge at church, became real in my codependent recovery. The relationship I had with God was different while growing up than the one I have with Him now. The church I attended as a young girl is different than the church, I am a member of now. My God is no longer a judging God, but a God I can have real short conversations with. When I say I have a relationship with the God of my understanding, I do. Letting go and letting God, was me learning how to surrender my will over to God, my higher power. I learned I have control over nothing. I learned the Serenity Prayer and it gave me focus on what was in my control and what was not. I could only change me. People, places, and things, other than myself, are not in my hula hoop. I learned acceptance of things I may not like, and needed to practice acceptance if I wanted to move forward.

If it were not for my sponsors that I have had in my codependency group, those in my church family, my mother, my sister, and my brothers, I would not have kept on keeping on. These people are my support system. As much as they are here for me, I hope I am there for them. I could not get through this life without them.

My command is this: Love each other as I have
loved you. ~John 15:12

Teresa D. Johnson

Teresa D. Johnson is an insurance professional, a blogger, author, and entrepreneur who resides in Taylorville, Illinois. Johnson was born in central Illinois and lived in Florida and Texas for a short time when she was young. It was during her time in Texas that she discovered her talent for writing and won first place in a statewide academic essay competition at the University of Texas in 1982. She later graduated with a Bachelor of Arts degree in journalism and political science. She freelanced for the Springfield Business Journal, a monthly business publication from the fall of 2001 to January 2016.

Connect with Teresa at https://linktr.ee/officialtimewithteresa.

CHAPTER 22

Finding Joy in the Journey

Tiffiny Jewel Roper

After losing my twins, Braden and Karissa, at twenty weeks pregnant, I had to find a way to move on, to heal. An "incompetent cervix" issue had forced my body into early labor with otherwise healthy, growing babies. The grief was overwhelming, and I didn't know how to move on. I struggled with where to start healing. Every day, anytime I was alone or falling asleep, I had constant flashes of memory of this horrific loss spinning through my head, on automatic repeat. I mean, how could the world go on without my beautiful babies? How could I? Where do you start when you don't know how to make it through an hour or a day...when you can't stop crying?

I held my sweet babies, alive, in my arms for three and four hours, not able to do anything to help them. The feeling was horrendous, such despair. I watched them struggle, and slowly die. They weren't able to breathe on their own because their lungs weren't fully developed. I held them as their heartbeats finally stopped. I was their Mommy, and I was supposed to protect them and keep them safe. After so many years of struggling to get pregnant, I had already felt like I wasn't "woman" enough to get pregnant without help. We conceived these babies through IVF (in-vitro fertilization). I knew women that had had miscarriages when there was something wrong with the baby, but I'd never heard of anyone losing perfectly healthy babies (outside of abortion). I, as their Mommy, felt I had failed them.

When I was at the hospital, after birth, I lost so much blood that I had to have a blood transfusion. I asked the doctor what would happen if I didn't have the transfusion, and she said I would go home and probably have a heart attack and possibly die. I remember thinking, "that sounds good, then I can be with my babies again." I didn't want to go on, to continue living without them. I decided to get a blood transfusion for my family, despite my feelings. Later that day, the day of my babies' birth and ultimate death, the nurse brought in my babies, covered in a small white blanket, and said, "take as long as you need to say goodbye to them." I immediately thought to myself, "how much time is enough?" How do you say goodbye to these sweet, super tiny, yet perfectly formed and beautiful babies? To my surprise, they even had fingernails, eyebrows, and eyelashes. I remember sitting with them, holding them, talking to them, apologizing to them for not keeping them safe, for having failed them. I told them how much I loved them and always would. I cried over them, watching my tears fall onto the blankets covering them.

Going home with empty arms to a house that was being prepared for babies, with a book the hospital gave me called *"Empty Arms"* (in case I had forgotten), was heartbreaking. I wondered why the world was still spinning around, and I was mad. How dare the world go on when my babies were no longer a part of it? I kept reliving the whole experience; the feeling of giving birth, of the babies leaving my body, watching them slowly die as I held them. A few days later, we had the funeral. I didn't know how to do that either. How do I say my final goodbyes? The funeral itself, while dealing with the emotions of others hurting at the funeral, was very difficult. Standing by my babies' tiny casket with my husband, reading a poem I wrote for them, watching everyone's tears fall around me, knowing this was really goodbye, was too much.

After the funeral, people went back to their regular lives and expected me to go back to mine. However, I didn't know how to go on. My whole world flipped upside-down and I was truly in pain and suffering. There was no more "normal." I rarely heard from anyone after that; people felt like they had "done their job" by going to the funeral, while I was struggling all day. My head was often filled with horrible memories, over and over, on a never-ending cycle. My heart felt so very heavy. It felt like an elephant was sitting on top of it. I didn't know how to stop hurting so much. One night I was so overwhelmed with the grief and pain I lay in bed and begged God to take some of my pain, to help me hold it because I wasn't strong enough to take it all on myself. Thankfully, the next morning, I did feel lighter. I was still in so much pain, but it was the first day I felt like I could finally start my healing journey.

For a couple of weeks after my babies passed, my husband, Avinash, was amazing and sat with me for hours as I cried, and he held my hand. Then, after about two weeks, I could tell he was ready to move on, or maybe he decided to tuck away his pain to keep going in his own way. I saw him play video games a lot more, and I knew that if I kept going to him with my pain, I would be bringing him down and keeping him from moving on. It made me feel guilty. Thankfully, I had my amazing dad, who was willing to talk to me for hours into the night, despite his own health issues, anytime I needed to talk to someone or I needed to cry. At one point, I went to a therapist, just trying to figure out how to survive after that first week of loss, and all she could tell me was "just cry." That was her answer? Nothing against therapy, but I could tell she hadn't been through it, and she truly didn't understand or empathize with my pain. At the end of the session, I felt worse. I never went back to her. Then, I found an infant loss support group where there were other couples that were struggling with a similar loss. My husband didn't want to attend the classes, so my dad offered to go with me, so I wasn't alone. I never asked him, and I thought I would be okay going by myself, but he truly knew me better than I knew myself. He was there for me when I desperately needed it.

Attending the support group, even though we all had lost our babies in different ways, was helpful to talk about my loss and know I wasn't alone. I also found an internet group for women that had lost babies because of an incompetent cervix. It was the most helpful thing, talking with other women who had lost babies in the same way and reason I had. I knew they understood. Later, I reached out to women who had just gone through their loss to help them, like others were helping me. I met some amazing, strong women in that group and attribute it, and my dad's unwavering support, to why I have my sanity today.

I learned a lot of lessons during this time of my life. I learned to take it one hour at a time, then one day at a time. I learned to find support, so I didn't feel alone. I learned to reach out to others and support them, so I could get out of my own pain for a second. Although, I was also living through it again while I helped them get through their loss. Often, I've found, the way to heal ourselves when we are suffering, is to help others who are also suffering. In addition, I found that I had to create boundaries with some people who said painful things to me. While they thought it was helpful, it wasn't. When someone loses a child, through miscarriage or otherwise, statements such as "well, they are in a better place" (better than mommy's arms?), or "you can always have another child" (so if you lose your spouse or an adult child, should I say the same?), are very hurtful. So many people don't know what to say, so they just stay away, which makes the person grieving feel even more alone.

So, what's the best way to handle it? If someone is grieving, there are often no words that will make them feel better, so know it is fine to just say nothing. Or you can say, "I know there are no words to make this better, but I want to just be here for you," then sit with them and hold their hand and shoulder some of the pain, so they don't have to bear the weight of it all on their own. Also, I learned that men and women grieve losing a child in different ways and timeframes. It is estimated that eighty percent of marriages will divorce or separate after losing a child. My belief is that it's partially because they aren't giving each other the grace or understanding that we grieve differently. Grace and kindness, not blame and shame, is the way forward, if you want your relationship to survive such a loss.

After a needed surgery and a few months, we were pregnant again with amazing twin girls. After such a traumatic loss, I was terrified. Every day was scary. I struggled getting through the first trimester, often the most dangerous one, but knew I still wasn't safe. Previously, my loss was in the second trimester. This time, I had to know I was going to get through it. The big mark to hit, this time in my pregnancy, was twenty-eight weeks. On that day, I was truly elated. I knew if my babies were born then, they would most likely survive. My dad was so happy for me, even though, just days before he had fallen and broken his rib and was in a good amount of pain.

On day twenty-eight and one day, out of nowhere, my dad passed away. He was my heart, my strength, everything to me. I was, and always will be, *"Daddy's Girl."* He was one of the main reasons I had held on and survived the loss of my babies. He was there for the worst day of my life, and I felt I owed him the best day of my life: the day my girls were born. My pain was immeasurable. How do I say goodbye to the man that made me who I am, the man that role-modeled what a loving, giving father looked like. Someone to look to when raising my own daughters. Now he was gone, unexpectedly. In less than a year, I was planning another funeral, and I was in utter shock.

Only a couple of short months later, I was having my beautiful babies, Avery Jewel and Sophia Madison. Meeting my girls was the best day of my life and truly felt like a dream. A dream that I thought, for many years, would never come true. I remember looking in my babies' eyes and seeing how deep their souls were and immediately knew love like I had never known before. The same love my dad had for me. In losing my dad, I had to learn his love didn't go anywhere, it was just in a new form. It was a form of energy I needed to get to know and feel in a different way. Now, I see my dad in every yellow butterfly that passes by me, in front of me, leading the way when I am on a path or driving, always watching out for me and my girls. I asked my dad, after losing my babies, if he would take care of them in Heaven, until I got there. These days, I know my dad is in Heaven, enjoying being a Papa to my babies and loving them and playing with them.

When my girls were two days old, I started feeling like I couldn't breathe when I laid back to breastfeed. I had panic attacks after losing my babies, and my sister thought I may be going through another one. They did x-rays on me, and days before Christmas, I learned I had postpartum cardiomyopathy, heart failure caused by my pregnancy. One-in-fifteen thousand pregnant women have this, after my one-in-one hundred diagnosis of incompetent cervix, and I couldn't believe it. My girls were taken away from me in the hospital, and I was moved to a different room and put on oxygen for twenty-four hours. After my diagnosis, I was told I needed lots of sleep and couldn't have any stress. I laughed, through my fear, telling them I'd just had twins, so wish me luck. My precious girls liked to take turns getting up every two hours. That allowed me to take care of one of them at a time, but that also meant I only got about thirty minutes of sleep a night. At that time, they also told me I'd need a heart transplant within five years, and the average lifespan of a heart or lung transplant patient was about five years, so I may not live long enough for my girls to turn ten. I was, again, in utter shock. My family helped me with my girls as much as they could. One sister, Michelle, had her teen daughter, Ashlea, stay the night to help for a few weeks. My other sister, Jennifer, took the babies overnight a couple of times with her girls. My mom, Jeanne, came a few times and watched the babies, while she barely slept, so I could get a little rest. My brother, Shane, would often call and check on me.

After getting used to the medications, and working up to exercise again, and slowly getting my ejection fraction back to a more tolerable range, I started feeling like there was some hope for a longer life. I am grateful and proud to say my amazing daughters just turned ten a few months ago, and I am still here, without a heart transplant.

Through all of the pain I've been through, I had to find a reason why I was going through it. For many years, I couldn't understand why I had gone through so much. I just had to trust, one day, it would make sense, so I could move on. When I really started focusing on my personal development, I started realizing why I had gone through the pain I had gone through. Though I'd always been a very empathetic person, having gone through the grief I had, feeling like I had no interest in continuing my life, and having to get through that to where I am now, I realized it was going to make me a much better person and Life Coach.

The thing missing from the therapist I went to, after losing the babies, was the fact that she hadn't been through something similar. She really didn't get it, and I could feel that. With everything I've been through, I have no doubt I can help others get results. With that, and the twenty years of project management experience under my belt, I know how to keep clients accountable to stay on track, and believe in them and their new possibilities, until they believe in themselves as well. These are all necessary skills for clients to reach their goals.

It's so important to find your purpose, your dream that will bring you true fulfillment and joy. My dream finally came true, becoming a Mom, and I am now motivated by my amazing girls to be the best Mom I can be for them. I continue to grow and learn, so I can be the role model they need to be confident, strong female leaders when they are grown and to inspire others to do the same. There was a dark time, during all of my pain, that I was willing to give up, but I knew I had to keep fighting for my family. I am forever grateful for their strength and belief in me when I didn't have it for myself. If I had given up, I wouldn't be where I am now, with my beautiful girls and serving others by helping them reach their goals and find the joy again in their lives. It's so important to surround yourself with those that will truly love and support you, that will lend you their strength and belief in you when you don't have your own. You need to have true friends that love you, raise you up, and want your happiness as much as they want their own. You also need to look at who is in your inner circle, that you spend the most time with, and start cutting out those that don't support you this way.

I've been through a long journey, but I wouldn't change anything. Despite the pain, I am who I am, the Mom and the Life Coach, because of what I have been through. When you have those dark days in your life, I hope I can inspire you to also never give up, to just take one step toward a compelling future and find your own joy again. There is always a better tomorrow, and if you have a breath in you, there is always hope. I know you can also find joy in the journey to the brighter days ahead.

Tiffiny Roper

Tiffiny Roper is on a mission to create confident female leaders of tomorrow that this world desperately needs. She accomplishes this as a Life Coach for Moms of young daughters, working passionately with them to reach their goals and becoming the confident role models their daughters need. In doing so, they live with a new purpose-driven life filled with joy and inspire those around them to do the same, starting with their daughters.

Tiffiny uses her twenty years of Project Management experience to keep Moms accountable in hitting their goals. She's also a speaker and best-selling author that loves creating memories with her husband of twenty years and young twin daughters, Avery and Sophia, including coaching their softball team and leading their Girl Scout troop.

Connect with Tiffiny at
https://www.facebook.com/groups/girlmomcoaching.

CHAPTER 23

Whatever Tomorrow Brings, You'll Be There

Virpi Tervonen

"I want that," I was silently saying to myself.

I was sitting among a small audience, gathered in a rented room in one of the many buildings in Singapore's business district. We were seated in folding plastic seats, each of us attentively listening to the speaker at the front of the room.

We were there, hopeful to hear the direction that would lead us to something we all wanted ... More freedom. Mostly freedom of money and time.

That was me. I was crystal clear and fully committed to starting my own business. Alas, I had no idea what it would be.

So, I signed up for the course they were selling. It was either called *Be Your Own Boss* or *Make Your Own Money.* Cliches, I know. But perfectly accurate in describing what I and others, who signed up for the program, desired for.

I remember one thing that they emphasized in that program: *Just do something!* Retrospectively, it's a vague piece of advice. After all, it's a transition from being an employee with a steady paycheck to being self-employed with no guarantee of income!

Regardless, I joined a work-at-home business opportunity that I found online. I was so determined to make that business a success that I promptly quit my job at the University.

That happened twenty years ago. Today, I understand the shock some people expressed. I was a first-time mother of a baby girl, fresh out of maternity leave, had recently moved to the other side of the world, to Asia, to continue my promising post-Doctorate career as a biomedical researcher. I had moved my family from Finland to Singapore for that job. Quitting it after a few months wasn't a rational decision, I admit. It wasn't even a well-thought-out decision. I made the decision to get away from the uneasiness I was feeling in the new job, and the expectations to work exceedingly long days with a long commute. I made the decision due to a strong desire to be at home, and be more available to my precious baby girl. It was an urge to do something new with my life in the new country, where I felt free from the societal and cultural expectations typical of Finland.

So, I do understand it was shocking to some. Furthermore, I understand why some people laughed in my face when they heard about my plans. I really didn't know what I was doing. But I was determined that I would figure it out. I was eager and willing to learn anything I had to. I believed that I would make it work, if I just worked hard enough.

Not so surprisingly, my first business venture wasn't a success. Little money dribbled in; enough to whip up my desire to make more of it. Earning more money became critical when the then-husband lost his job. Instead of trying to find another job, he chose not to. "I want to stay at home, like you," he explained.

I became the sole breadwinner for our family. I couldn't have done it without our full-time helper Nemy, who took care of the household and looked after our daughter. She was just a little bit over one year old at that time.

It's fascinating how my subconscious motivators - namely to be strong and independent, and smart and knowledgeable - drove my choices and actions to a direction that furthermore provided me options to be strong and knowledgeable. Until all the available choices demanded me to be strong and independent, and smart and knowledgeable, even if it was beyond my capacity to be that. It wasn't just my subconscious motivators, but also my inner Saboteurs that had a remarkable impact on my thinking and behavior.

Our commonly known, but little understood, mental enemies.

Our Saboteurs cloud our discernment, and cause us and people around us unnecessary unhappiness, and misery. They harness some of our natural strengths and coping methods into a controlling system that appears to help us. In reality, they undermine our innate capabilities, such as empathy, curiosity, openness, innovation, navigating our life's path, and taking focused action.

My strongest Saboteurs, Avoider and Hyper-Achiever, had a significant impact on what options I was able to see, what kind of decisions I made, and what kind of action I took - or didn't take.

Characteristic of people with a strong Avoider Saboteur is that they tend to avoid things that appear difficult to them. They avoid conflict, even if it means saying yes to things they don't want, and downplay the importance of real problems, in an attempt to maintain harmony or balance.

People with a strong Hyper-Achiever Saboteur have a high need for constant performance and achievement for self-validation. However, joy from any achievement is fleeting and self-acceptance seems to constantly hide behind the next achievement. I'd describe having Avoider and Hyper-Achiever as the strongest Saboteurs feeling as comfortable as driving a car with one foot on the gas and the other on the brake pedal. They cause inner resistance, friction, and discomfort that consumes loads of energy and mental bandwidth. (Discover YOUR strongest Saboteurs at SaboteurTest.com)

Having learned these things about myself, it makes it easier to understand why I accepted the full responsibility of supporting the whole household on my own so easily. Occasionally, I felt proud of how much responsibility was on my shoulders and how much I was doing to provide for my family.

In reality, I was efficiently burning my candle on both ends. I was working hard to grow my business and manage household matters, while constantly feeling guilty for not being the mother I wanted to be. I wasn't spending plenty of time with my daughter to build a wonderful relationship with her and create memorable moments that she'd cherish. That was difficult to do from the Saboteur-led state I mentally was in. I would mostly think of work, no matter what else I was doing. I believed that I could be the person and mother I wanted to be, only after I had attained success. I also believed that *if it was to be, it was up to me.* It is a belief that turned me inwards instead of being open to help and support. To live up to that belief, I was pushing myself to work harder, do more, faster. If I couldn't, it was a sign for me to toughen up, put my head down, and solder on.

Self-criticism, denying satisfaction, and threatening ourselves with worst-case scenarios can seem like an efficient way for us to motivate. Especially when they work. They do, to a point. What we don't realize is the actual cost of a negative mindset. It stops us seeing the bigger and more impactful outcomes we could have created, if our mind had been operating from the Sage-led stage, instead of the Saboteur-led one. Little good comes from choices, decisions, and actions taken in a Saboteur-led state. It consumes us and our wellbeing, and negatively impacts our relationships and people around us, leaving us little life to truly enjoy.

The entrepreneurial freedoms

Most people think that the main motivation to start a business is money. It isn't. Money is the means to something more important ... freedom.

Those who start businesses do it with no guarantee of success or even income, because they are motivated to have more freedom. The founder of Strategic Coach, Dan Sullivan, names four different varieties of freedom: Freedom of Money, Time, Relationships, and Purpose.

I began to get a sense of what Freedom of Money was, when my business income exceeded what I earned as an employee. I realized that my income was not tied to years of experience or limited with salary brackets. This, my first profitable business, was an Information Marketing business selling eBooks.

My training as a science researcher turned out to be useful in launching and building the information marketing business. It was exhilarating to do keyword and market research that revealed what people wanted and to what extent the demand was fulfilled. When I identified a niche topic with a high volume of searches and low number of quality search results, it was an opportunity for me to provide that information. I bought or borrowed a few books about the topic from the library, studied them, wrote an eBook, and made it available for a fee. The topics varied from beekeeping and cake baking to acupressure massage, and thus, I was publishing these eBooks under a variety of pen names.

My timing with my eBook business was great. Increasingly, more people were getting used to making purchases online and they were willing to pay for a digital book in the form of a downloadable PDF instead of receiving a hard copy in mail.

In addition to creating the products from scratch, I also built the websites for each of the products myself. Dreamweaver software was the most advanced WYSIWYG (what you see is what you get) website development software and I used it to build my first few HTML websites. When WordPress became available, I learned how to create WP sites for my niche products.

Getting traffic to my websites was another set of skills I became good at. I learned SEO (Search Engine Optimization) and even got certified as an SEO expert. Backlinks and articles were big SEO elements at that time. I wrote loads of articles and published them on sites like eZineArticles and Squidoo. Adding paid traffic from Google AdWords increased the targeted traffic further.

I worked hard, but I also got rewarded for my efforts. Everything seemed to work great, and the revenue kept increasing so quickly that I began dreaming of becoming an Internet Millionaire! So, I doubled down to do more of what I was doing: bought more keyword rich domain names, put up SEO optimized niche websites, and created more eBooks.

Everything is temporary

When things are going great, we want to believe it's always going to be that way. The truth is that change happens. If we are not able or willing to adjust accordingly, some of the good will come to an end. This happened with my eBook business. The global financial crisis 2007-2008 happened and it had an impact on my sales. Google made a major algorithm update and it was strongly unfavorable to my niche website rankings, making them sink down in search results. Bidding for keyword placing at Google AdWords became expensive for tiny businesses like mine, selling low-priced products with no upsells. Finally, the number of sites competing on the same keywords increased, and some of my best-selling products got modeled after or copied. All that killed growth and the eBook business began to wither.

I panicked. Instead of becoming rich, I was going broke. My then-husband suggested that I'd get a job to support the family, and so that he could stay home. It didn't sound sensible to me. Furthermore, I had gotten a taste of entrepreneurial freedom, and I liked it. The idea of getting a job was revolting.

The eBook business had assets, such as almost one hundred keyword-rich domain names, a couple of dozens of optimized niche websites with a product, each of them getting organic traffic. And a subscriber database of over 25,000 people. The deep sense of failure that was made worse by harsh self-criticism blocked me from seeing value in what I had built. Because I had been doing most of the work alone and had not developed a network of peers and mentors, there was no one to help me to shift my perspective. So, instead of even trying to monetize the existing assets, I let all of it crumble away.

My solution was a new business model that was trending at that time: small business online presence building. I was capable and qualified to help local small businesses get their website up and optimized. However, some businesses wanted more than just a simple website. I had to hire people to do website graphic design and development. With that, I stretched too far out of my level of capabilities. Managing people in my team, dealing with the demanding customers, and disappearing developers was not what I had prepared for. It was messy and stressful.

Then I got lucky. A prospective client wanted business coaching instead of online presence services. We had a conversation about what she wanted from coaching and I said, yes to the opportunity. The work I did with her was a mixture of mentoring and consulting, rather than coaching. But the client got great outcomes, better outcomes than she had hoped for. The next two coaching clients seemed to appear almost from thin air, and working with them turned out to be successful, too. Achieving desired results while doing something that feels natural and energizes you is a solid sign that you have found your playground. It felt incredible to have found mine!

Since working with my first coaching client ten years ago, I have developed my professional skills with certifications in Business, Executive and Mental Fitness coaching. I have created coaching programs for entrepreneurs who want to develop themselves, increase the value of their company, and have a business that is less dependent on them.

The freedom to choose with whom I work with has given me amazing clients, and fantastic peers to collaborate and become friends with. I love the freedom to do work in which I get to make a positive contribution using my natural strengths and conative skills. I find what I do purposeful. If I ever grow out of this current purpose, I am confident that I'll find a new one, if there are future seasons requiring such a transition.

When looking back is good for you

Many times, life may turn out in ways you least expect, regardless of your effort to create something else. Those periods of life can feel overwhelming and demanding for any person.

It's a common saying that you should not look back, but focus on the future. I disagree. If you don't look back at past events, you are going to miss a great opportunity to distill richness from your successes, mistakes, and failures.

You can better understand how you created your successes and hence you can use that wisdom to replicate and multiply your successes. Also, failures can be transformed into gifts of knowledge, inspiration, or power.

My lessons to share with you

1) Embrace necessary endings

Never giving up isn't about never quitting anything. If you resist necessary endings, you'll get stuck. Starting a new phase in your life, or getting to another level with your business requires ending something and leaving it behind while moving on. The new phase might have a different purpose and value priorities. If we don't accept endings and manage them well, the improvement or growth that we are seeking will never materialize, whether in terms of advancing our businesses or improving our personal lives.

2) Think about where the energy comes from

When you want to start something new or create a bigger impact, think about where you'll get the energy to do that. You can preserve your energy by using the wisdom your procrastination provides, and get someone else to take care of the activities that take a lot from you to get them done. Developing professional relationships plugs you into a network of energy. Neglecting relationships is a poor strategy. This includes the relationship with yourself. Get to know your strongest Saboteurs, how they steal your energy, and then improve your mental fitness to stop that from happening. Entrepreneurial freedom allows you to build a business in which you can focus on using your natural strengths and do things that re-energize you. You actually can do what excites you and get paid for it!

3) You are not alone and all is not dependent on you

We have rather amazing capability to overcome challenges and navigate through rough patches of life. Our resourcefulness helps us to get through transitions, and our ability to renew our minds, identity, and purpose helps us to thrive in different seasons of our lives.

When we feel lost and disconnected, it doesn't mean that we are. Often, we are at the right place, but are just not familiar with it. At times, there seems to be no progress. You, however, don't need to be constantly pushing things. Take your rest and trust that God is doing her part as is promised. Always remember, whatever tomorrow brings, you'll be there.

Virpi Tervonen

Virpi Tervonen, the Certified Executive & Mental Fitness Coach for Entrepreneurs. She has talent for concocting unique strategies, seizing opportunities, and fearlessly navigating complex issues.

Founder CEOs seek her transformative powers to banish self-doubt and cultivate a healthy confidence. By amplifying their company's value and creating businesses that thrive independently of their founders, Virpi helps them reclaim a higher quality of life.

As the mind behind the acclaimed 'Mental Fitness for Entrepreneurs' and 'Upleveled Leadership' coaching programs, Virpi has been coaching Founder CEOs across diverse industries since 2011. With over a decade of personal entrepreneurial experience dating back to 2005, she brings a unique perspective to her coaching approach.

Virpi has credentials in scientific research, including a Ph.D. in Physiology and BioPD in Biotechnology, yet her zest for life has always extended beyond the confines of the lab. Splitting her time between Singapore and Finland, she loves being a mother to her accomplished daughter who's pursuing her studies in Finland.

When Virpi isn't helping entrepreneurs conquer their business challenges, you can find her socializing with friends, breaking a sweat through exercise, immersing herself in captivating movies, or embarking on exciting adventures.

Connect with Virpi at www.realrelevantresults.com.

Afterword

As we conclude this remarkable journey through the pages of "Never Give Up: Stories of Perseverance," we are humbled and inspired by the unwavering spirit that each author has shared with us. The tales of triumph over adversity and the resolute commitment to never giving up serve as a powerful reminder that within each of us lies the potential for greatness.

The stories within this anthology are a testament to the human capacity for growth, transformation, and unyielding determination. From the moment we embarked on this project, it was clear that the threads connecting these narratives were not just tales of success, but of resilience – the kind of resilience that propels individuals to continue moving forward even when faced with challenges that seem insurmountable.

Throughout these pages, we've journeyed alongside entrepreneurs who turned failures into stepping stones, artists who channeled setbacks into creative fuel, and individuals who confronted their fears with unshakeable courage. We've witnessed the transformative power of perseverance – a power that has the ability to reshape destinies and illuminate paths that were once obscured.

As we close this book, let's remember that the stories shared here are not isolated incidents but reflections of the human experience. Each story is a reminder that challenges are not to be feared; they are opportunities to embrace growth, to redefine success, and to evolve into the best versions of ourselves.

We want to extend our heartfelt gratitude to each contributing author who shared their journey of resilience. Your stories have the potential to ignite change, inspire courage, and serve as guiding lights for those who may be navigating their own paths of perseverance.

To our readers, thank you for embarking on this journey with us. As you put down this book, we hope you carry with you the spirit of never giving up. May these stories serve as a reminder that every challenge you encounter is an invitation to push your boundaries, to tap into your inner strength, and to emerge stronger on the other side.

Remember, you have the power to shape your story, to transform challenges into triumphs, and to navigate the path of life with a resolute spirit of perseverance. Let these stories be a source of inspiration as you embark on your own journey of resilience.

With deepest appreciation,

Lynda Sunshine West, Founder & CEO
Sally Green, Vice President of Author Development
Action Takers Publishing

READER BONUS!

Dear Reader,

As a thank you for your support, Action Takers Publishing would like to offer you a special reader bonus: a free download of our course, "How to Write, Publish, Market & Monetize Your Book the Fast, Fun & Easy Way." This comprehensive course is designed to provide you with the tools and knowledge you need to bring your book to life and turn it into a successful venture.

The course typically **retails for $499**, but as a valued reader, you can access it for free. To claim your free download, simply follow this link ActionTakersPublishing.com/workshops - use the discount code "coursefree" to get a 100% discount and start writing your book today.

If we are still giving away this course by the time you're reading this book, head straight over to your computer and start the course now. It's absolutely free.

READER BONUS!

ActionTakersPublishing.com/workshops
discount code "coursefree"

Manufactured by Amazon.ca
Acheson, AB

13257754R00146